BASEBALL'S LAST GREAT SCOUT

TEAM CINCI Reds   COACH   DATE 4/13-2 21-37

NO.	NAME	POS	AGE	HT	WT	CL	B	T	A	F	R	4	P	
21	DEION SANDERS	8	✓				L	L					Y	Great
11	BARRY LARKIN	6	✓				R	R					Y	Great
23	HAL MORRIS	3	✓				L	L					Y	Good
6	RON SANT	7	✓				R	R					4	OK, Leg ok Good
16	REGGIE SANDERS	9	✓				R	R					Y	Good
29	BRETT BOONE	4	✓				R	A					Y	Good
12	Willie GREENE	5	✓				L	R					?	CHANGE
10	Eddie TAUBENSEE	2	✓				L	R					4	OK
19	JEROME WALTON	8	✓				R	R					NO	AAA OR EXTRA MAN
22	Thomas HOWARD	9-7	✓				5	R					4	Good Extra man
~~38~~	~~~~	-												
20	JEFF BRANSON	H.6 p/s	✓				L	R					NO	Conflict Some + Good Extra
30	BRIAN Hunter	7-3	✓				R	L					NO	OK Conflict
68	JERRY BROOKS	pH	✓				R	R					NO	Not enough - AAA
17	Benito SANTIAGO	2					R	R					NO	OK

Form 313

Baseball's Last Great Scout

THE LIFE OF HUGH ALEXANDER

Dan Austin

UNIVERSITY OF NEBRASKA PRESS | LINCOLN AND LONDON

"Make Your Own Kind of Music": Words
and music by Barry Mann and Cynthia Weil.
© 1968, 1969 (renewed 1996, 1997) Screen
Gems-EMI Music Inc. All rights reserved.
International copyright secured. Used by
permission of Hal Leonard Corporation.

"You're Gonna Hear from Me": Words by
Dory Previn, music by Andre Previn. © 1965
(renewed) Warner Bros. Inc. (ASCAP). All
rights reserved. Used by permission.

All photographs are courtesy of the National
Baseball Hall of Fame Library, Cooperstown,
New York, unless otherwise indicated.

Library of Congress
Cataloging-in-Publication Data
Austin, Dan.
Baseball's last great scout : the life of
Hugh Alexander / Dan Austin.
pages   cm
ISBN 978-0-8032-4501-3 (cloth : alk. paper)
1. Alexander, Hugh. 2. Baseball scouts—
United States—Biography. 3. Baseball—
United States—History. I. Title.
GV865.A334A87 2013
796.357092—dc23
[B]   2012032832

Set in Lyon by Laura Wellington.
Designed by Nathan Putens.

This book is dedicated to "Uncle" Hughie Alexander and to the past and present generations of baseball scouts, whose invisible works become apparent with every spring training.

All royalties from the sale of this book are donated to the National Baseball Hall of Fame and Museum in Cooperstown, New York, in honor of Hugh Alexander and the thousands of scouts who unrelentingly look for the players who will fill the rosters of professional ball clubs for the next generation of fans.

CONTENTS

ACKNOWLEDGMENTS

This book began with a simple phone call to Hugh in the early 1990s to talk about his then fifty-three-year scouting career. Immediately after the first meeting, Hugh and I talked about writing a book.

"A lot of guys want to write a book about me, but I want you to do it. Is that a promise?" Hugh asked. "We're both midwesterners and can trust one another."

"Yes," I replied. "We'll do it."

For over seven years we met infrequently at Hugh's ranch near Brooksville, Florida, or spoke on the phone to record his memories, delightful and studied insights into scouting. He reveled in remembering his early years as a scout in the late 1930s, culminating with his work with the Cubs sixty years later. Just a few months before his death, we had dinner together. He was weakened by cancer, but however unsteady his gait, he remained cheerful and optimistic.

The tape recordings of our meetings, as well as Hugh's scouting reports, are now in the library of the National Baseball Hall of Fame and Museum. Only with these conversations would this book be possible. His trust in me to record and transcribe them is deeply appreciated.

I want to gratefully acknowledge the assistance of the following persons who provided interviews about Hugh Alexander in his youth and during his scouting career: Bob Alexander, Gladys Alexander,

Acknowledgments

Dick Calmus, Ron Clark, John Dawson, Jerry Fraley, Jim Frey, Doug Gassaway, Fred Goodman, Billy Grabarkewitz, Dallas Green, Derrell Griffith, Charley Joseph, Jack McKeon, Pam Warren, and Carl Warwick.

Thanks also to Hal Leonard Corporation, Warner Brothers Inc., and Warner Chappell for permission to reprint song lyrics and to the National Baseball Hall of Fame Library in Cooperstown, New York, for their photographs.

A special thanks to my attorney, Lee Anne LeBlanc, who diligently worked to identify the copyright holders of the song lyrics and gained permission for them to be printed in the book.

The following sources provided additional information about players, managers, and baseball executives: Baseball-Reference. com; National Baseball Hall of Fame Library, Jim Gates, librarian; SABR Baseball Biography Project, http://sabr.org/bioproject; Baseball-Almanac.com; *Seminole (OK) Producer*; MLB.com, History; *The Baseball Encyclopedia*, 10th ed. (Macmillan, 1996); *The Official Encyclopedia of Major League Baseball*, 4th ed., edited by John Thorn and Pete Palmer with Michael Gershman (Penguin Group, 1995); Leonard Koppett, *Koppett's Concise History of Major League Baseball* (Carroll & Graf, 2004); Bill James, *Historical Baseball Abstract* (Villard Books, 1988); *Branch Rickey's Little Blue Book: Wit and Strategy from Baseball's Last Wise Man*, edited by John J. Monteleone (Macmillan, 1995); *The Sports Encyclopedia: Baseball 2007*, edited by David S. Neft, Richard M. Cohen, and Michael I. Neft (Griffin, 2007).

To the staff of the University of Nebraska Press, especially Rob Taylor, Courtney Ochsner, and Sara Springsteen, and to Joy Margheim, I extend a note of thanks for your due diligence and patience with me.

Lastly, I hold my wife, Nancy, responsible for continually reminding me about the promise I made to "Uncle Hughie" to write a book about his remarkable career. Her insistence and confidence opened doors to the baseball world hitherto unknown to a kid who grew up in Kansas and continues to this day loving the game of baseball.

BASEBALL'S LAST GREAT SCOUT

Introduction

Baseball's Last Great Scout is the poignant, funny, and high-spirited story of Hugh "Red" Alexander, a baseball scout for sixty years. Growing up in the oil fields on the outskirts of Seminole, Oklahoma, he felt the sting of the dust storms, the rancid smell of oil, and the bites of grasshoppers during the Great Depression. None of these scourges kept him from playing baseball, basketball, and football and running track. Some say he was a born athlete, excelling in all sports. After high school he packed his glove and spikes and headed to North Dakota to play ball, unlike the thousands of Okies who fled west to California.

A stubborn, hardheaded redhead, he did have the good sense to listen when it counted. With all the gifts of an athlete and pampered as Oklahoma's answer to Jesse Owens, he still counted only on baseball to make a living. Being a track and field star didn't pay the bills in the 1930s.

As a ballplayer and a scout, he pursued both jobs with the same level of dedication and preparation. He loved the high drama of the game; he realized its tediousness and recognized that in all its beauty, it could also be brutally painful.

"How do I judge a ballplayer?" asked Hughie rhetorically. "Whatever talent stops me in my tracks." Like other scouts over several decades, he followed the fads and the revolutionary changes in the game. Sometimes he scouted for speed; other times he looked for hitting for power or improved bench strength. Always he hunted for pitchers, not unlike today. What he stubbornly searched for, unrelentingly, was knowing the heart and the attitude of a player.

Hundreds of books have been written about the baseball greats. Fans have opinions about who is the greatest center fielder or the best fielding third baseman. What has not been extensively written about is the lesser-knowns of the baseball world, the overlooked and underappreciated scout. He's the one who looks at a kid and makes a decision about his ability to make it to the Big Show.

Scouts, a small band of invisible men and now women, have populated the grandstands for decades. They remain unnoticed except by hopeful managers and aspiring players. It is tempting to put scouts at the periphery of the game. But they are the ones who fill the club rosters five or six years hence and, hopefully, fill the grandstands for another generation of fans.

I embarked on a journey with Uncle Hughie in 1991, while interviewing some players, managers, and umpires who played during the midthirties through the midfifties for the National Baseball Hall of Fame. Bill Guilfoile, then a vice president of the Hall of Fame, asked me to interview Hugh, as little information had been collected about scouts. At that time Hughie had been a scout for fifty-three years, working with five different clubs and serving under every baseball commissioner from Judge Landis to Fay Vincent. (In 1992 Bud Selig became acting commissioner.)

Hughie became a scout out of necessity, adversity, and love of the game. After finishing his second year in baseball as an outfielder, he returned to his home a few miles east of Seminole. In December 1937 his left hand was ripped off by water well cog gears, ending his playing days. Within three months he embarked on a scouting career, the youngest scout in Major League history.

The word *scout*, according to Dan Schlossberg's *Baseball Almanac*, appeared in baseball language in the 1840s, identifying the position behind the catcher. A scout grabbed pass balls and wild pitches and fielded hits. In that era a batter could run on balls falling anywhere in foul territory. Hughie had the speed and quickness to be a scout, whether behind the plate, on the pitcher's mound, or in center field. From 1991 until early 2000 Uncle Hughie and I met several times to record his rich experiences. He wanted the baseball world to know that he signed more players who made it to the Major Leagues than any other scout and that he spent sixty-two exciting years in professional baseball. In 1998 Hugh retired as director of player development of the Cubs. A heavy smoker, he was in ill health but still remained active, offering advice to other scouts whenever sought. In November 2000 he died and was buried next to his parents in Seminole, Oklahoma. Ten years earlier, in 1990, a sports complex was named in his honor and he was recognized as Scout of the Year of the Major Leagues.

Every team he worked for was a winner or on the threshold of becoming a winning club. Beginning with the Indians in 1938 through 1952, then with the White Sox from '53 through '55, switching to the Dodgers in their next-to-last season at Ebbets Field, making new beginnings in 1971 in the front office with the Phillies, and concluding his career with the Cubs from 1987 through 1998, Hugh offered a cross-country guide to baseball's places to see. From a solitary American Legion field in Anadarko, Oklahoma, to a tryout camp in Kilgore, Texas, to a beer joint near Baton Rouge, Louisiana, Hughie had his loyal contacts to find new talent for the big leagues.

He traveled the dirt roads of Oklahoma and Texas and then headed to the blacktops of Louisiana and Arkansas, winding northward to Kansas and Nebraska. Hughie became a road scholar of baseball looking for the next Jimmy Foxx, Walter Johnson, and Lou Gehrig. Hobnobbing with bartenders, coaxing a tip from an American Legion coach, but always keeping his sources close to his chest, Hugh labored in the vineyards of the Midwest for over thirty-five years and then headed to the front offices of the Phillies and Cubs for over twenty-five years.

He planned every signing, every trade, and every negotiation.

He grew up knowing one thing: "If I'm going to compete, I want to win. It makes my work fun." He loved to beat back opponents and test conventional wisdom.

He considered himself a sterling example in the fraternity of scouts. He did his homework. He carried no stopwatches or radar guns, nor did he load the car trunk with golf clubs. While some scouts took a few summer afternoons off for golf, Hughie chased a few more leads a hundred miles down the road.

Hughie's reputation did not end with signing players. He earned the respect and admiration of general managers and managers. He taught others to become scouts and helped general managers appreciate the art of trading. Tough, savvy, outspoken, he challenged rules and tradition. Yet he worshipped tradition and became outspoken about the amateur draft system.

It's up to the scout to keep fans coming to the park. Baseball fans want excitement and entertainment at the park. Happiness is a beer and a hot dog mixed with a stolen base or a bunt sacrifice. Being at the park breaks life's doldrums and offers relief from the drudgery of everyday work.

In 1938 there were but sixteen Major League clubs, with St. Louis the farthest west. In 1998 thirty clubs existed from coast to coast. In 1938 all players in the Majors were white. By the end of the twentieth century the rosters were integrated, with African Americans, Hispanics, and Japanese.

What did not change in those six decades was the need to find ballplayers with the tools of the trade and with the right attitude to perform. That was Hughie's job: to find the proper mix of talent and attitude for the next generation of fans.

1

A Stick of Dynamite

It was a cold, raw afternoon on December 5, 1937. Working on an oil well water pump near his family's home in Cromwell, Oklahoma, Hugh "Red" Alexander thought about his debut with the Cleveland Indians only three months earlier. A "stick of dynamite" his teammates had called him since his high school days. Fast, powerful, and cocky, he had the numbers to live up to it.

Called up by the Indians in late August, he had spent most of the time on the bench with a few chances to pinch-run. In three months he would be off to the Indians' spring training camp in New Orleans, but now he was helping his parents do some repair work around their home in the middle of an oil field.

Working on the water pump, he thrust his hand down into the shaft to adjust the cog gears. Suddenly his shirt sleeve was caught by one of the gears, dragging his hand into the churning machinery. He felt a sharp jerk on his left arm. Looking down, he stared momentarily in disbelief and then let out a bellowing scream. His left hand, nearly ripped off, lay enmeshed in the gears. Blood spurted everywhere. His mother, standing nearby, heard him.

"Oh, mother, my hand! It's caught!"

Finally freeing his hand, his mother rushed him to the hospital in Seminole. After an intense examination, the doctor said there was no hope for saving his left hand. He proceeded with the amputation.

The next morning, lying in a hospital bed, the twenty-year-old Cleveland rookie told a reporter from the *Seminole Producer*, "I don't know yet just what I'll do." His mother stood at his bedside with tears in her eyes. "I think I will go on to college and study coaching. I haven't heard anything from Cleveland yet, but I expect to this afternoon. Cy Slapnicka will wire as soon as he hears about it."

Four months earlier he had gotten off a train in downtown Cleveland, just shy of his twentieth birthday. He had made it to the Big Show with just under two years in the Minors. Fiercely determined, he knew that it would not be just for a cup of coffee. With a wiry frame, packing 180 pounds, he felt cocky and bullheaded and ready to collect the rest of his $1,000 bonus, with $250 already in his pocket.

The Indians had kept their eye on Hughie. Cy Slapnicka, the scout who signed him and was now general manager, knew he had three of the five tools of the trade—running, throwing, and hitting with power—and he proved it in the Minor Leagues.

Now, lying in the hospital bed, he thought his career was over. A one-handed kid with no other job skills in the midst of the Great Depression invited only misery, and not much optimism. Certainly there would be no more headlines in the local newspaper, no more slaps on the back by well-wishers, no more home runs, and no more stolen bases.

However, there was one other thought that entered his head: his parents, Harry and Mae, would not tolerate his feeling sorry for himself. Yes, it was a shame that his playing days were over, but he was young and had a whole life ahead of him.

Hugh Alexander was born on July 10, 1917, in Lead Mine, Missouri, a wide space in the road about forty miles northeast of Springfield. Five years later his parents, Harry and Mae, packed up their belongings and three children and moved to Cromwell, Oklahoma, about fifteen miles northeast of Seminole, to work in the oil fields. His parents knew hard work growing up in the Ozarks. Farming was a tough and unforgiving business, especially there. The soil was so depleted that if you wanted to raise crops, you had to haul in dirt. Even the high agricultural prices during World War I did not spread to the farmers of southern Missouri. Corn, oats, and tobacco became dependable cash crops if there was enough rain and no grasshoppers.

Oklahoma (formerly Indian Territory), which achieved statehood just ten years before the Alexanders' arrival, offered a new beginning. Oil wells had already cropped up around Blackwell, Oklahoma City, and Seminole. Black gold meant jobs, and thousands from Missouri and Arkansas poured into the state looking for any kind of work.

Harry, Mae, and the kids found housing immediately. They lived in a tent, called company housing, in the midst of an oil field. Harry took a job as a roughneck, digging ditches and laying pipe. Mae took care of the kids, cooked for the workers, and did their laundry using a scrub board and lye soap.

No one in the Alexander family or their neighbors knew even rudimentary luxury. Hardship enveloped each day in the oil fields. Nearby farmers at least could grow their own vegetables and tend to the family cow. In the oil fields nothing grew, not even weeds.

Kids learned hard work quickly. Scrubbing socks and underwear, then wringing them and hanging them out to dry was a Monday ritual. By age five, everyone had chores, even if the work was perfunctory. One of Hughie's first jobs was cleaning the globes of the kerosene lamps.

In central Oklahoma, where romantic writers describe how "the winds come sweeping down the plains," keeping house with an open doorway was sheer drudgery. The flaps of a tent were the only barrier against dust. Even when the Alexanders later moved to a house, dust constantly sneaked through every window and doorway. Every kid learned quickly about dusting furniture and washing curtains.

Company rules forbade workers to leave the oil fields to eat their meals. On call twenty-four hours a day, seven days a week, workers never knew when a well would blow or a fire would break out. If they ran off to town, they might not return to work sober. Rounding up a bunch of guys in beer joints or in shacks with prostitutes in the alleys behind took too much time and could prove just as dangerous as putting out a fire in the fields.

Kids in the oil patches grew up on their own while the parents worked. The oil fields became their playground. They played ball, hide-and-go-seek, and other games. The red clay, thickened with runoff crude oil, was as slick as a slab of marble and tough on the body when sliding into "home plate" next to an oil rig.

A game of cowboys and Indians meant fashioning their own toys. From the worn-out leather bands on the rigs, they made pea-shooters. Nuts and bolts served as pellets to shoot at one another or to kill rats rummaging through the garbage pits.

One day Hughie shot his brother "Doc" right between the eyes as he peeked from behind a rig. He fell unconscious and all the kids thought he was dead. They dragged his body over to a tapped water pump to revive him, but when they turned on the valve, the water pressure almost tore off his face.

Cromwell had only a one-room school house. Most children didn't go to school beyond the eighth grade, as they were then old enough to get a job and help the family. Every morning a bunch of kids, well-scrubbed and with a bowl of hot oatmeal and a teaspoon of cod liver oil in their bellies, ran off to a clapboard building with two outhouses to learn reading, writing, and arithmetic.

A kid's education did not end with the school bell ringing at four o'clock in the afternoon. Harry and Mae, although working twelve to fourteen hours a day, meted out a demanding discipline at home.

Mae, a deeply religious woman, didn't tolerate cussing from the children. One day Hughie's brother Doc let out a barrage of profanity, and immediately Mae seized him by the collar and marched him over to the bucket with water and lye soap to "rinse" out his mouth.

Hughie muttered, "I'd like to see her do that to me."

Mae jumped over a chair and dragged him over. "Don't you ever think you're bigger than me!"

Hughie had the makings of a rugged individual, but his mama was boss.

By the late twenties Harry's determination and entrepreneurship got him a promotion to field supervisor. Now, for the first time in six years, they lived in a wood-frame house. Yet the tough work continued for both him and Mae, raising kids and chickens, washing and darning clothes, and fixing meals.

They expected their children to learn quickly about how to work. Harry's rule: when you look big enough, you start working. At age ten Hughie worked in pool halls learning how to play poker. A hustler, he gloated at beating someone out of a quarter. If someone had offered him a diploma, it would have read, "Bachelor of Arts in Street Smarts." He didn't have time to think about the hard, scrubby life. No one else did either. Work meant sweat; if you weren't sweating, then you weren't working.

The way to survive was to be resourceful. In town he cut grass, and when in high school, he lived at the fire hall. He cleaned the movie theater every night for help pay for his room and board. On a good night he made a dollar. Like most Depression kids, Hughie thought that no matter how much money he had in his pocket on one day, the next day he could be broke.

Like his father, Hughie wanted to be in control. His sister and her friends loved to dance, not something that captured his imagination, so he decided to be a manager of dancing contests in Seminole. Arranging the music and dance hall, he collected the admission and charged a handsome commission, something that irked his sister Edith and her friends. However brusque he may have been, Hughie charmed people with a disarming smile and tall tales, traits that he carried with him the rest of his life.

In the early thirties Harry bought a saloon in Seminole, where Hughie worked. Within a few seconds a saloon could change from a low-key atmosphere to hostilities. One night a drunk, slovenly and loud-mouthed, challenged Hughie about the price of a quart of beer. "Twenty-five cents, like hell. I'm paying you only a dime, you little SOB!"

Hughie picked up a billy club from behind the bar and clobbered him.

"If you're going to fight, throw the first punch," was Harry's advice to all his boys.

Other than drinking, a poker game in the darkened rear of the saloon invited the regulars to stick around. As with all other saloonkeepers, part of the action belonged to the house. No one ever said much about the rule. It was just understood.

Of course, a drunkard would easily forget the rule or get greedy, as often happened. One night a drunkard hit Harry over the head with a beer bottle, shattering the bottle and cutting him across the forehead and cheek. They struggled on the floor. Finally Harry grabbed the drunkard's ear, sank his teeth into it, and bit it cleanly off his head.

Headstrong and cocky, Hughie loved to challenge orders. When he was a teenager, his parents decided to visit some relatives in Missouri. Harry drove his car, and Mae's car remained at the house with its key under the control of Henry, Hughie's older brother.

As soon as they left town, Hughie told his brother that he was driving the car to town.

"No, you're not, Hugh!"

"Yes, I am!"

After a few more words, Henry pulled out a penknife and stabbed Hughie in the left knee. (One needed the left foot to operate the clutch pedal.) The bleeding did not stop, so Henry drove Hughie to the doctor's office in Seminole. The doc stitched him up, wrapped a bandage around the wound, and sent him home.

"Now you better not be hobbling around when Mom and Dad get back home or I'll tell them what you tried to do, Hugh," Henry ordered.

Hugh obeyed, and it wasn't until six months later when Mae went to town that she accidentally saw the doctor who treated Hugh. "How's Hugh doing?" the doctor asked.

"What do you mean?" she answered. Then she heard half the story. Returning home, she learned the rest of the story.

If the twenties proved burdensome for the Alexanders, the thirties brought the apocalypse. By 1934 a drought spread misery beyond the memory of any living Americans. Dust rolled up on the horizon. The years of drought and over farming the land now harvested misery. The scene spawned despair and the novel *The Grapes of Wrath*.

In the early thirties Hughie, better known as "Red," witnessed the Great Trek unfolding. Folks piled some bedding and clothing atop their black Model A, children hopped into the back seat, and they simply left their land. To reclaim a farm wrecked by wind and buffeted by economic forces appeared beyond hope. They just picked up and headed west for a new beginning in California. The Alexanders remained in Cromwell, working in the oil fields.

Seminole, like all boom towns, had a surplus of three ill-gotten commodities: guns, booze, and prostitutes. Life was tough and raw. Most people carried guns strapped around their hips, and armed posses roamed the streets at night to protect their belongings. Even in the twenties and early thirties, streets remained unpaved. After heavy rains, mules dragged their bellies in the piles of mud, pulling wagons full of machinery and food.

However poignant the lives of many Oklahomans were, children mustered a resilience to survive. Everybody struggled. No one escaped suffering. It broke some people's spirit and determination. Life just continued one day at a time, day after day after day. As Hugh's parents reminded the Alexander children, if you play it smart, there's nothing you can't do, and don't let anyone tell you differently.

In earlier years Harry had publicized himself as a boxer and took on all comers who arrived in town, especially the carnival people. In late spring and summer carnies spread across the Midwest, paying hawkers to spread the word about them coming to town. One troupe included a 250-pound behemoth advertising himself as a world champ. If anybody could stay in the ring for more than one round, he won ten dollars. Harry took them on.

The odds of any "boxer" collecting a bounty were nil, except for Harry. He knew how to survive in the ring, getting a lot of experience in some beer joint brawls, and it was a quick way to pick up a few bucks.

Harry wanted to know what was inside his son's head. Did Hugh (Harry always called him "Bill," as he never liked his given name) have any guts to stick around? So he decided to put him in a boxing ring with bruisers forty to fifty pounds heavier. That was the first test.

"Now, defend yourself, or I'll beat the hell out of you. You're fast. Start skipping, dart in and out. Big guys can't move. They got lead in their ass." If Hugh didn't mix it up, Harry would outline a boxing "ring" in the dirt, put on some boxing gloves, and get into the ring himself.

Yeah, Harry taught his son to fight! That's right. "Bill, that's when people respect you. You're quick and strong. Dance around them. With your speed, you'll wear any 250-pounder out in three rounds. Protect your territory, and then give him the sucker punch. That's the plan."

Hughie surprised everybody. Fast, wiry, and cocky, he wasn't scared of anyone.

Within a few weeks Red made his boxing debut as the first carnival hit town. Harry put up the entry fee. The cash pot: five dollars if the local stayed upright in the ring for one round, ten dollars for two rounds. No one in recent memory had ever collected a dime, despite town bullies, assorted juvenile delinquents, and star athletes taking a stab for a quick dollar.

Red made some good money, and by late summer everybody knew about him. Just before one fight with a big purse, Harry took him aside. No one would ever suspect a scrawny teenager tampering with the rules of the game.

"Bill [Hughie], I'm goin' to wrap your fists [even as a teenager, Hughie's fist was half again as big as a man's] with tape and then tape a band of steel to your knuckles. Keep your mouth shut. After you knock him out, just get out of the ring and leave. I'll collect the money later. Understand that!"

He won a few pots. No one in the crowds suspected him, but the carnies did, as he darted out of the ring each time and ran behind the tent to have Harry get rid of any tainted evidence. Word got around the carnival circuit not to let Hughie get into the ring. Well, he made some good money while it lasted.

Always find a way to beat your competitor. Harry kept beating the idea into Hugh's head. He taught Hugh to be aggressive, but with a smile. Know people's names, know their weaknesses and strengths and what they like and don't like if you're going to be around them for a while. You just never know when an old customer or rival will reappear.

Harry got his break working with a wildcat oil company by buying mineral rights from farmers. His tools of the trade: an envelope full of cash, legal descriptions of each farmer's land, blank contracts, and a fountain pen.

Harry talked like a seasoned traveling salesman, always looking for a deal to sign. Undoubtedly, Hugh picked up a lot of pointers from his father to use later in his scouting career. "Just sign here on this piece of paper. You got it made."

Convincing farmers to sell their mineral rights, Harry roamed the countryside earning a reputation of never taking no for an answer. Farmers couldn't afford to drill for oil, and they probably would be stuck with a dry one anyway. "Here's the deal," he'd say as he pulled some green bills out of his pocket. Holding the money in his hand, Harry found that it cut out a lot of unnecessary talking.

A farmer and his wife trying to raise a bunch of kids on the dusty prairie saw instant relief. Seeing all that cash on the kitchen table brought a moment of hope. *"Cash is hot!"* Ain't that America? *Cash* is the name of the game.

This was Hugh's world when he entered high school. His trump cards: his athletic ability and Harry's uncanny conniving. Even as a ten-year-old, folks around Seminole heard about his speed. He was faster than all the other kids his age, so he played football and baseball with guys five years older. Hell, that wasn't hard. Gifted athletes matured early.

Once he began high school, the trip into Seminole took a lot of time. After school he hopped a ride home. That routine left no time for sports. Apparently Harry had thought about that predicament and began inquiring about finding a place in town for Hugh to stay during the week.

An accommodating fire chief had the answer. Hugh could stay at the firehouse across the street from the high school. He would do odd jobs around the place and sleep upstairs with the firemen. He soon had a new home. That was to be home five days a week for three years.

Harry told the fire chief to keep an eye on Hughie, but any curfew was not enforced. The "rope" around him was pretty lax. By the winter of his freshman year, he became a street urchin, a twentieth-century Oliver Twist, but without a Fagin to beat him. His life became a struggle between freedom and restriction. Unlicensed freedom was usually the winner, until it got him into trouble.

He loved to do his own thing. Why listen to anybody else, as nobody could compete with him on any field? He had a big mouth, cussed like a sailor, but most of the boys he ran around with did the same thing. Calling someone a "son of a bitch" was like yelling "hello." Sailor talk, that was all it was. If a preacher or a pretty girl talked that way, they would have been run out of town.

He tried out for football and made the team. He exploded like a "stick of dynamite," breaking loose from a tackler for another touchdown. "Paced by a Red-Headed Stick of Dynamite, Seminole High School Wins the State Crown," read the headline.

In one game he averaged 25 yards per carry, ending up with 6 touchdowns, 6 extra points, and 505 yards. Every time he got the ball, he scored. (In those days there was no free substitution. When the coach took a player out of the game, he remained on the sidelines for the rest of the quarter.)

With about a minute left in the game, and Seminole High leading 45–0, Hugh ran out of bounds on purpose and handed the ball to the coach.

"What the hell are you doing, Red?" the coach shouted.

"I'm tired. I just quit. I've been running all day." Maybe the song "Catch Me If You Can" belonged only to Hughie.

During his junior year he was elected captain of his football, basketball, baseball, and track teams. He was fast! He ran the 100-yard dash in just under 10.0 seconds. (Jesse Owens held the world record at 9.6.)

By his junior year a couple of semipro teams in Oklahoma City heard about Red's exploits on the baseball field. They needed his speed and power hitting, so he was able to pick up a few bucks. Playing for five bucks per game, that was good Depression money. Nobody squealed on him. A lot of guys got money, and they were still in high school.

In one doubleheader, he blasted four home runs. A few days later he hit two doubles and two home runs. Already by age sixteen he was a *ringer*. Twenty-something guys looked up to him. Everybody needs to hold on to something, to believe in something or someone. Hugh believed in himself. When he ran out on the field, his teams became winners. No, there was nothing humble about him. He had the right stuff. And he wanted everybody to know his name.

Hugh was the talk of Seminole and nearby towns. Fans of all ages slapped him on the back, waved from across the street, and laughed at his every joke. As his fame grew, so did his bragging and cockiness.

2

Enter Cy Slapnicka

It was while Hugh was playing semipro ball that scouts began noticing him, including Cyril "Cy" Slapnicka of the Cleveland Indians. Hughie never saw any of them and wouldn't have recognized them anyway. Probably his high school coach or one of the semipro managers fed his name to Slapnicka. Slapnicka had a big reputation among coaches in Oklahoma and Texas, and they always fed him tips about the latest hot prospects.

Slapnicka began working for the Indians in 1923 and in 1935 became vice president, serving in that position until 1941. He pitched in the Minor Leagues for eighteen years, from 1906 to 1920, with two brief trips to the Majors, in 1911 and 1918. Pitching for the Cubs and Pirates, he won one game and lost six. As a scout he "discovered" Bob Feller and Herb Score. (He left the Indians in late 1941, worked with the Browns and Cubs, and returned to the Indians in 1947 at Bill Veeck's insistence before finally retiring in 1960.)

One night he searched out Hughie to talk about playing professional baseball. Hughie just listened to how he could make some decent money playing a game he loved. In the Depression days that offer seemed distant and remote, until he heard it directly from Slapnicka.

Oklahoma was a hotbed of raw athletic talent. Every high school boy in the area read about Jim Thorpe, who grew up in Pottawatomie

County. The 1912 Olympic decathlon and pentathlon gold medalist and later Hall of Fame football player stood on a pedestal of athletic achievement.

A few select boys received athletic scholarships to go to Aggieville (Oklahoma A&M, later Oklahoma State) or to Norman (University of Oklahoma). Big men on campus sporting letter jackets came back home to tell high school kids about college life. If you were an athlete, you could get a good ride.

Hank Iba, baseball and track and field coach at A&M, then known as Mr. Baseball, had his contacts to learn about outstanding athletes in the state. High school coaches paid homage to him and quickly informed him about up-and-coming athletes. Hugh Alexander got on the list.

Iba made a pitch to Hughie to play baseball at A&M, but Hughie turned him down. Not many high school kids rejected a personal offer from Coach Iba. He told Hughie about some great opportunities in college and about the upcoming 1936 Olympics.

Hughie listened to Coach Iba and finally told him that he had to make some money. There was no money in track and field or in college baseball. Only professional baseball offered him a chance to make some good money within a couple of years.

"Don't do it!" Iba pleaded. "Come to Stillwater and in a year you'll be on the Olympic team with Jesse Owens. Besides, you'll get a college education."

"Well, I don't like track anyway," Hughie replied. "What the hell! I'm going to sign up [with the Indians] if I can."

Later Hughie, never gun-shy about speaking up for himself, told Slapnicka, "I need some money. When I sign, I'm going to lose my meal ticket at school and my room at the fire hall."

"Okay, I'll give you $250," Slapnicka replied.

"I need more than that," Hughie countered without hesitating.

So Cy wrote out in big letters on a Big Chief school tablet, "If you make it to the big leagues with the Indians, I guarantee you $1,000. [Signed] Cy Slapnicka."

A few weeks later Hughie reported to spring training in New Orleans. The Indians assigned him to their Fargo, North Dakota, farm team, where it doesn't become springtime until mid-May. And even in June the temperature can dip into the forties. Hughie soon discovered the tingling of a bat in forty-degree weather and the difficulties of living far from home.

He played in every game with the Fargo-Moorhead Twins. The team traveled all over the upper Great Plains to play against such teams as the Sioux Falls Canaries, the Wausau Timberjacks, and the Winnipeg Maroons.

After a game the team would hop into an old rickety bus and ride well into the night to another town like Jamestown to play the Jimmies. To pass the time away, Hughie would pull out a deck of cards and invite four or five to join him in a few hands of poker, penny ante. Just throw in a few pennies. With a quick shuffle of the cards, he would lure a few to stay in the game. After a couple of hours, he would have tomorrow's meal money. A game of poker, like golf, tells you real quick-like the kind of man you're competing with.

On the bus players would sleep straddling the aisle or against someone's shoulder, trying just to get a few minutes of uninterrupted sleep, then be awakened by screeching brakes as the bus stopped in front of some flea-bitten hotel.

During the Depression, baseball was the glue that held small towns and surrounding areas together. Chambers of Commerce praised the hometown teams, offering free tickets to kids and free admission to women on Saturday afternoons. Knotholers got in for five cents. No better entertainment than to go to the ballpark on a summer's day just to shout for the home team.

Hughie always remembered with pride the invitations to come to a fan's home for dinner on weekends. Most of the players had never been away from home, and it was just a few days after the season began that Mom's cooking began to occupy many an idle thought while sitting in a strange greasy spoon on Main Street. Eating fried chicken and biscuits drowning in white gravy with a heap of mashed potatoes, finished with some homemade blackberry pie put them back into a good frame of mind. It was a grand way to pick up morale. Even answering a kid's questions about baseball did not deter grabbing another drumstick.

A player's eating allowance was about a dollar a day. By supper time, little money was left for dessert and a modest tip. So hunger pains stayed around all summer long.

It was a good league in those days, Class D, just for rookies, the lowest classification in professional baseball. Only in the higher classifications did youngsters meet a veteran of five or six years, just trying to give it one more shot before packing up and going home.

Most of the managers were first-rate guys. The Twins manager treated everyone like his boys. He made sure they obeyed curfew and wrote letters to the folks back home. Long-distance calling was too expensive. Besides, it took a few hours just to place a long-distance call with an operator.

Sometimes players got reprimanded, but in a caring way. A severe talking-to took place behind closed doors, where it was expected to remain, not even discussed with teammates. Within a few hours everyone knew what had happened, but nothing was spoken.

The biggest enemy was the amount of time with nothing to do. Just sitting around a hotel lobby or in a locker room—sheer boredom—waiting for the clock to tick away another hour. After a day game, a few walked around town and maybe headed for the movie house, as much to see some pretty girls as to see a B cowboy movie.

Ballplayers did not read much except for an occasional pulp detective magazine. They just didn't say to a teammate, "Hey, let's go to the library." Rather, the pool hall became the hangout to sneak a beer, a place of great familiarity to Hughie.

Hughie learned quickly to have a quick tongue. No one would out-talk him. Growing up in the oil fields and a beer hall taught him to size up a man quickly. Harry, his father, preached unrelentingly to get the first punch or word in. When Hughie opened his mouth, his teammates stopped to listen. Instinctively, he wove a story line about a special game or player, but always with a novel ending. He damn well wanted them to remember everything he said. Add some cuss words, make the story flamboyant, and add a few colorful guys—the elements of deal-making later in his career.

Hughie batted .348, drove in more than 120 runs, and hit 28 homers in his first year. He even got a few headlines in the local paper and peppered his interviews with the sports reporter (who also wrote the obituary column and wedding announcements) about being the fastest kid in Oklahoma. Yes, there were even a few stories made up just to let everyone know that Hugh was also a fast talker.

The last week of the season Slapnicka arrived in Fargo. "You're going to be a good ballplayer," he began. He carried a bag like a lady's purse and began pulling out some cash and counting it. He stopped at $600. "Do you know how much that is?" he asked.

"Yeah," Hughie replied. "$600."

"Well, I'm going to give it to you to tide you over this winter, 'cause you're some kind of ballplayer."

On September 24, 1936, a day after Hughie returned home, he took part in the field day program at the Seminole-Ada baseball game. Sheriff Vance, business manager for the Redbirds, arranged the exhibition game with the Kansas City Monarchs, the famous traveling Negro Leagues team. Patrolling the outfield, Hugh showed the townspeople why he belonged in the Major Leagues. The following morning he put on his work clothes to work in the oil fields.

The next spring, 1937, Cleveland sent Hughie to its Springfield, Ohio, club (Class C) in the Middle Atlantic League. In four preseason games, Hugh hit six home runs. He let it be known that nobody was going to stop him.

He hit Class C pitching well, traveling to cities in Ohio, West Virginia, and Pennsylvania. Farm clubs owned or affiliated with Major League clubs were still relatively new, most of them established in the early twenties by Branch Rickey, who later became general manager of the St. Louis Cardinals. Other clubs picked up on the trend quickly.

Long bus rides remained, as they had the preceding year. That was the hardest part of playing in the Minors. Only teenagers and young men in their early twenties could endure the grind and monotony of long, seemingly never-ending bus rides.

In 1937 he played about eighty games with Springfield, hit .344, clobbered 29 home runs, and knocked in more than 90 runs. A leader on the team, he led the league with a slugging percentage of .715. In mid-August Slapnicka told him to pack his bags and get on the next train to Cleveland.

When he arrived at League Park II, Hugh dared Slapnicka with the question "Why did you call me up so soon? I didn't play enough in Springfield. I could have hit a few more home runs."

"No one in Cleveland," Slapnicka retorted, "believes that a nineteen-year-old kid has hit fifty-seven home runs in two seasons. I decided to bring you up to see if you are really that good."

Cocky and outspoken, Hughie was going to prove to the Indians that Cy Slapnicka made the right pick. Hugh Alexander was already "some kind of ballplayer."

Now he was in the Big Show, and he meant to stay there. Bob Feller was already the hero in town, and the Indians were pennant contenders, giving the Yankees and the Tigers some solid competition.

Oscar Vitt, the Indians manager, gave Hugh a brief welcome and introduction to the team. Just a few words and that was it. Quickly Hugh learned that Vitt was either loved or hated by the players. There was no neutral ground.

Hughie had only job: to show everybody that he was the best. Played sparingly for the last month of the season, he sat on the bench most of the time. He played in seven games, getting one hit in eleven times at bat. Well, at least he was wearing a Major League uniform.

Earl Averill played center field, rookie Ken Keltner was at third, and Feller, Denny Galehouse, and Mel Harder rounded out the starting pitcher corps. Sitting on the bench, Hugh saw some of the greatest ballplayers of the modern era, a lot of future Hall of Famers, including Joe DiMaggio, Lou Gehrig, Bill Dickey, Hank Greenberg, Mickey Cockrane, and Charlie Gehringer.

The oil rig accident ended his baseball career just two short months after he donned the Cleveland Indians uniform. Now Hughie lay in a Seminole hospital bed with no left hand. The local newspaper wrote about his tragedy. High school buddies circled around him for a short time; then in a few weeks the visitors dwindled. No more headlines proclaiming the hometown hero. No more applause. No one seemed to care about his heroics on the field. Wisely, Harry and Mae bluntly told him that he wasn't going to sit around and feel sorry for himself. Their advice: just thinking about the accident would lead only to trouble. There was nothing that was going to bring his hand back, and all his baseball buddies would soon return to their own routine, leaving him alone to decide his own future.

After getting out of the hospital, he wandered around town and began drinking too much and coming home drunk. His parents again spoke bluntly to him. He was not going to live in the house drinking beer and smoking cigarettes every day and then hang out with the wrong guys at night.

After a couple of weeks recuperating, Hughie finally took up bartending again. Quickly he learned to plug beer kegs and wash and dry glasses with one hand and his "club," as he labeled his left arm.

He was going to do things by himself. Nobody was going to beat him at his new ball game. Label it "rugged individualism," he simply intensified the desire to succeed. "Trailblazer" is a more appropriate label to describe him. He had a handicap, but it never stood in his way. Nor did he let anyone define him as handicapped person. Those were fighting words, as some unfortunate souls found out.

Just before Christmas, the phone rang at the beer joint. One of the workers answered. "It's long distance for you Hughie."

"Hughie, how're you feeling? What are you doing?" Hughie recognized Slapnicka's voice. Before Hugh could answer, Slapnicka continued, "Hughie, you're about to become a baseball scout, and if you agree, the $1,000 bonus is yours."

"Hell, I don't know anything about scouting," Hughie replied, remembering that rarely did he admit any ignorance about sports.

"Well, you're about to learn," Cy emphasized. "What you lack is only the experience of making bad decisions. What you do have is the guts and drive to be a good scout. I'm sending you a train ticket. Get here [to Cleveland] as fast as you can."

Hughie's face brightened. The glimmer of a smile drifted across his face. He saw a new chance. It was a helluva better deal than feeling sorry for himself in a beer joint in Seminole.

He didn't know what would happen next, but it had to be better than anything during the past month. He was returning to baseball with skills he didn't know he had. A big learning curve lay ahead.

3

On the Road Again and Again

How would Hughie describe his first year of scouting in 1938? The answer: he didn't know what he was doing. Playing baseball and scouting talent seemed to involve opposite worlds. As a player he had the talent and delivered on the field. He knew what kind of ballplayer he was, but how could he figure out what talents and attitudes another player had? Within a few weeks after spring training, he was going to find out. He knew that he had a lot of learning to do.

In early February he drove down to New Orleans to meet with Cy during spring training. The Indians held spring training at the ballpark of their Class A-1 Southern Association club, the New Orleans Pelicans. New Orleans was some kind of town. It stirred the juices—a big party town. Dixieland jazz, fancy seafood that never hit central Oklahoma, and great barbecue.

"What do you want me to do?" he asked Cy.

"I want you to watch these players for ten days. I'll help you grade them. Then you're going back to Oklahoma and South Texas where the weather is warmer and work yourself north to the Canadian border by midsummer."

Spring training included a lot of guys on their way down and eventually out of baseball in a couple of years and several on their way up. Joe "Burrhead" Dobson, a pitcher from Durant, Oklahoma, not too far from Seminole, caught Hugh's attention. In 1939 Dobson made the Indians roster and stayed in the Majors for a number of years. Hughie liked his delivery. (Dobson and Hughie got reconnected in the midfifties with the White Sox.) Even a guy named Kit Carson made an appearance, but he didn't make an impression.

Cy pointed out a few guys who could make it to the Big Show. One was a pitcher, a Red Evans who showed a lot of stuff with the Pelicans later that year on his way to a 21-14 record. He later played with the Dodgers and the White Sox.

For a new scout looking for talent and establishing his name, Hughie quickly learned to look beyond the rules of the game and even the performance of a player in any given game. The Indians expected him to analyze what tools of the trade a player had and to predict what he was capable of doing. After all, Hugh would be spending the boss's money.

"Tools of the trade" is one of the enduring terms of baseball, yet it is fraught with misunderstanding and misuse. Cy, a veteran on and off the field, never assumed that any rookie scout had any understanding of the subtleties of the term. Even veterans had to check their own instincts when they watched a raw package of talent smack the ball out of the park or a dominating pitcher strike out ten or more batters a game.

"Hit with power" or "snag a line drive up the middle." Any amateur can see a home run or a sinking liner turned into a double play.

Cy warned Hughie constantly about knowing the difference between "performance" and "the tools of the trade." Oftentimes rookie scouts thought of the two terms as synonyms.

The tools of the trade embrace five skills:

hitting
hitting with power
speed (not the same as quickness)
fielding
throwing

If a player had two of the tools, mixed properly with a winning and hustling attitude, then he could make it to the Big Show. If a scout found someone with three tools, sign him up now.

Slapnicka and later Branch Rickey kept reminding Hughie to focus on execution, not just performance and results. You can see some kid go 2 for 4 in one game, thinking that was usual. He may have just had a lucky day, getting a flunk hit while putting his foot in the bucket.

A raw, overpowering pitcher whipping a fastball past inexperienced batters thrills the fans, but two months later he could end up with tendonitis because of poor mechanics.

Sitting in the New Orleans Pelicans' grandstand during 1938 spring training, Slapnicka unrelentingly questioned Hughie when observing a player.

How did the batter move his feet? Did the pitcher "square off" to the plate after his delivery? Did that speedy runner know how to slide into second base depending on where the baseman positioned himself to take the ball?

What Slapnicka was doing was converting Hughie from an amateur to a professional. Slapnicka knew the difference, but Hughie, a twenty-year-old novice, had barely a clue. A professional knows when he makes a mistake. He immediately identifies it and can give an answer to correct the problem. The amateur shrugs his shoulders in frustration because he sees only performance, not execution.

Not on the list of the tools of the trade but what every scout needed to know was what was in a kid's heart. He could be a ringer in his own hometown, but when he began competing with those just as good or better, the rookie needed the discipline to face some harsh reality.

When looking at a high school boy, one of the toughest jobs for any scout, Cy reminded Hughie, is to figure how he would do in mastering some of the tools three or four years later. Remember to study the boy's attitude. Does he hustle down the first-base line on a routine grounder to the second baseman? Does he run on and off the field? Check him out.

Jerry Krause, who scouted a couple of decades later, observed another point about a boy's attitude. "The toughest thing is to look at a high school kid hitting in forty-degree weather in April and project how he would do in the Bigs." Watch a kid behave under adversity.

Slapnicka and later Branch Rickey and Paul Richards, who managed the White Sox in the early fifties, preached the same message, but the latter two delved into the subtleties of analyzing which tools of the trade a club needed at different positions. Some clubs wanted speed and quickness, such as when Astroturf replaced natural grass in many parks in the early sixties. In the nineties hitting with power dominated the game. Learning what a club would need in a couple of years and spotting it on the field became the stuff of effective scouts.

Cy taught Hugh to observe the moves of a player. A scout can pick up a pitcher's release of the ball or a second baseman's snaring a sharp grounder and converting it into a double play. If a scout is lucky, he may even find a pitcher delivering a slider in an unorthodox way and making it work.

Hughie knew nothing about pitching. He played the outfield, far removed from the pitcher's mound. Cy took him aside and told him to look for a pitcher's control, his fastball, and his ability to field his position. Until the midfifties nearly all pitchers took a long, exaggerated windup, like Warren Spahn. Nevertheless, they didn't let their "high leg" wander aimlessly away from their body. That was a no-no. If they did, they could not finish up square to home plate.

If someone asked Hughie how a pitcher throws a baseball, he would have replied, "With his arm." He paid no attention to what part of the arm and the use of his legs. Cy pointed out at every chance, "A pitcher's got to use his forearm and wrist." That's the extra thrust. Otherwise you will sign a pitcher who will have a sore arm in a couple of months.

"Hughie, you gotta watch the way a pitcher uses his legs and different parts of his arm. If you're looking only at strikeouts and walks, then you're hurting us. And it's important that you look for a pitcher's release point. Does his arm come down over his opposite knee consistently?"

Another point Slapnicka emphasized: a good scout learns to look at a player with no preconceived notion about his being a pitcher, a shortstop, or a center fielder. Watching kids catch fly balls, throwing to first base or to a relay man, and hustling around the bases—those qualities become the first things to look at.

Baseball is a bottom-line business. Winning is what counts. Like the game of golf, it is the ultimate meritocracy. It's a beautiful game, but it is also ruthless and unforgiving, casting aside a lot of young men who couldn't handle the unrelenting pressure. They had a couple of the tools of the trade, but their brains turned flat on them.

In mid-March Hughie got into his Chevy and drove home. A few days later he hit the road for South Texas, still wondering how he could spot ballplayers with the tools of the trade. Slapnicka did give him one tip—stop in every town with a newspaper and ask the editor who the best high school or college player in the area is. If there was no newspaper in town, Cy told him to check with the local bartender.

Hughie met a lot of other scouts, all of them twenty to thirty years older than him. They lived hard, and it took only a few days for a twenty-year-old kid to follow in their footsteps. Scouts, like players, had lots of time on their hands. They sat around at a beer joint or in a hotel lobby swapping stories and drinking. Yes, Red, as most other scouts called him, began leading a fast life. He had to just to keep up with them, always trying to sign a kid, then moving to the next town like a traveling circus.

Always finding new ways to make some money on the side, Hugh would take one of the scouts into a side room. "Want to make a bet? I bet you that I can tie my shoes faster than you." He pulled back his shirtsleeve to show the stump.

"That's no bet. I got two hands. Sure, I'll take your money," the unsuspecting scout would yell.

Hughie beat everyone. It was a good game to play in beer halls and pool parlors, or even at the ballparks.

"Hey, kid, let me buy you a drink! What's your name? What happened to your hand?" Most conversations began that way when people first met him.

Sometimes, one of them barked, "Hell, I didn't know you were handicapped, Hughie."

The words seized in Hughie's head. With a snap, "I'm not handicapped, and no son of a bitch is going to call me that. I'll beat the shit out of him. You understand?"

The word got around. Don't call Hughie handicapped. He didn't think of himself in that way, and nobody was going to get by with it. Nobody, but nobody! Besides, how could a real handicapped person drive tens of thousands of miles with one arm, across Texas, New Mexico, Louisiana, and up into the northern plains?

A lot of scouts had their own "tools of the trade" in the car trunk—golf clubs. Hughie called them "temptation leading to unemployment," although he became a respectable golfer himself. On a sunny summer afternoon the golf course loomed as a powerful magnet to drag someone away from the ballpark. The excuse: "I can always see the kid tomorrow." But the tomorrows lead to a few days later or next week.

At a ballpark or local beer joint Hughie gathered-in occasional tips, but in those days one just didn't give away proprietary information. Hold your cards close to your chest. Only one club is paying your salary, so that's where the scouting reports are sent. You can drink with them, play cards, and "shoot the shit," but that's all. That's where the line in the sand was drawn.

Yes, he picked up a few hot tips, some from scouts with tongues loosened by too much booze. Maybe it was because Hughie was the "new kid on the block" and they much older that they could left down their guard and give him the name of an American Legion coach who knew how to evaluate players or the name of rising high school star.

Hughie began learning to guess, not wildly, but to make educated guesses about players and coaches anxious to push their stars. The thinking sounded relatively crude, but he learned that if he could not make up his mind about signing a player, "Walk away, walk away. You're spending the boss's money, so you gotta guess right."

What else did a scout need to know? He wanted to find out what made a player tick—his attitude, his guts, his hustle and spirit. If he heard alibis or not wanting to play every day, then a warning signal rang. Watch out! This kid can bring only misery.

Getting a kid's attention by telling him you worked for the Indians was tougher than Hughie imagined. The Cardinals and Yankees held a monopoly on kids' loyalties throughout the Midwest and South. The Cardinals offered small-town radio stations a chance to be in the big leagues, to broadcast the Cardinal games with local sponsors. Everybody becomes a winner. It didn't take long to figure that out. Both clubs captured the baseball headlines, but for different reasons: the Cardinals with their "Gashouse Gang" aura, the Yankees with a new era of Joe DiMaggios and Bill Dickeys.

Hitting the road with a full tank of gas and staying intent to follow up on the next hot tip. Those were the marching orders as Hugh hopped into his Chevy, heading out of town down another road. Many a day the wind blew reddish clay soil across the highways, coating everything with a thin veneer of dust. His mouth tasted dirt all summer, driving up and down the highways. By every late-summer afternoon he wanted to get to wherever he was going and find a hotel with a laundry room and a shower.

The prairie's horizon seemed endless, broken only by solitary white grain elevators and some cottonwood trees hugging the banks of a river. On a hot summer afternoon, Hughie approached a town that seemed to be just a few miles away, but even as he moved closer, it remained far away. He felt suspended in time and distance. Life appeared to move in slow motion under the glaring white heat of the afternoon sun. By four o'clock the wind kicked up, rolling tumble-weeds down the main street.

Hughie kept a diary during his first couple of years of scouting. The routine was straightforward, recording the names of towns, ballparks, and players. In McKinney, Texas, he wanted to watch a kid named Wafer pitch for the high school in early spring. But it rained.

Later that day he drove to Austin to see some college teams play. TCU and the University of Texas were first on his list. Already he had lined up some sources who told him to watch three kids—Layden, a left fielder with a good arm and fast, with some power; Deutsch, a starting pitcher; and Haas, a right fielder, a good hitter, fast, but no arm.

The next day he sought out a boy named Jennings on TCU's team. But he found out later that he was hurt and wouldn't be playing for a couple of weeks. Finally the weather cleared, so he watched the teams play. Texas center fielder Looney had lots of power, was fast, had a pretty good arm, and was worth keeping an eye on. Dumke, the Texas pitcher, was fast but so wild he couldn't find home plate.

A couple of days later, Hughie spotted a newspaper article about the McKinney High School Lions successfully defending their base-ball title. Their star pitcher, Wafer, who Hugh didn't see because of a rainout a few days earlier, struck out twenty-one batters. A week later Hugh was on the road to McKinney to talk with the high school coach about him. Hondo was the kid's nickname, seventeen years old, 175 pounds, and six feet tall. In a couple of years, Hugh figured, the kid would develop, so he asked the coach to keep him updated.

Once, near Tyler, Texas, Hughie kept his eye on a junior college second baseman. His coach remarked that he had the tools of the trade but still needed a lot of hitting instruction. Impatient at the plate, he often swung haplessly at a curve or change of pace. Hughie thought about his other skills and where he would fit in one the Minor League clubs. Although lacking at the plate, he showed hustle and determination. Someone to look at next year.

One of the toughest jobs any scout has is looking at a high school or junior college (JUCO) boy to figure out if he could make it. Scouting is always sifting through imperfections, winnowing out a couple of hundred kids, and then reducing the numbers even further.

The early summer sun boiled down on Hugh's back as he walked up the plank steps in the ballpark. A roof over the grandstand rarely greeted him except at a Minor League park. He squatted on a rough-hewn board warped by years of sun and rain. Splinters of wood, tapered like nails, meant no sliding around. There he sat, game after game, under the beating Texas sun. Another hot summer with scorching winds out of Mexico was in the forecast.

Despite rough patches of weeds in the outfields and unpredictable bounces, a ballpark invited serenity. The gentle flow of grass quietly led to wooden fences painted forest green. An occasional banner advertising a local bank or café flapped in the wind.

After two months, the back roads of East Texas began looking the same. Finding baseball talent was going to take some planning. There was no way he could cover every small prairie town, let alone believe every coach and newspaper account about the next great hitter or pitcher.

In late May he paused at a crossroads near the Oklahoma-Texas border to grab lunch. A Phillips 66 gas station and a beer joint with a blinking light beckoned the weary traveler. A sign swinging in the wind advertised "ethyl, 12 cents a gallon, beer, 10 cents a mug." He pulled up, filled up with gas, and drank a couple of beers.

He knew the world of baseball could be brutal. What if he failed? But the question quickly fled his mind. Rather, he thought, what would baseball people say about Hugh Alexander in ten years? He had to make some plans. Be aggressive, keep moving, and make contacts.

How should a scout approach his work? It sounded like a simple question, but surprisingly, just a few scouts had an answer. Hugh figured if he expected the kids he was watching to have a hustling attitude, he ought to look also at himself. Yes, he was a hard-driving young man, well honed in the oil fields and saloons.

After a few months on the road, he sat in a lonely hotel room writing a few commandments—maybe not ten of them, but at least some thoughts:

> I shall make plans. Be bold, be daring. After all, a young scout lacks only the experience of making bad decisions.
>
> I shall travel the dirt roads, gravel roads, and blacktops to see new players.
>
> I shall not whine. It's a time waster and won't win me any friends or sign me any players.
>
> I shall be lucky once in a while, but most of my successes will be plain old hard work, making personal contacts.
>
> I shall have a pair of well-trained eyes to spot the true mechanics of the game.
>
> I shall know the difference in a player who thinks "I shoulda made that last play" and "I woulda not gotten that last play."

Commandments easily become suggestions, forgotten, if not relegated to the back recesses of the mind. Slapnicka knew Hugh well enough that he had to bring his own set of rules to the young scout's attention, sometimes in public places.

Slapnicka often reminded him about the unwritten rules of scouting. They were deceptively simple, yet difficult to carry out. The first required scouts to have a plan to find the networks that know talent. It may be a coach or bartender. The second rule was to make only promises that you can keep, and then keep track of them. Write them down.

Third, know the player's mama. Treat her like a queen. She raised the kid, took care of him when he was sick, fixed his favorite food, and washed his clothes. She will give you an idea about how the boy will handle himself away from home.

Through the first week of July, Hughie spent nearly all his time in Texas and Oklahoma, watching Minor League players and then catching some semipro and American Legion games. Then he headed for Kansas, a hotbed of American Legion ball. Manhattan, Junction City, Marysville, and Topeka crowded his schedule, as he watched an afternoon game in one town, then drove fifty or sixty miles for a night game. Rainouts created a headache, but there was no sense complaining.

In Salina he spotted a tough, seventeen-year-old lefty pitching for the Salina American Legion club, Bob "Sugar" Cain from nearby Longford. Good fielding and speed and a strong arm. He had good habits and didn't drink, a good Christian boy. Making a note, Hughie promised to check up on him in a couple of years. (In 1949 Sugar Cain made his debut with the White Sox. Two years later he became part of baseball trivia when he pitched for the Tigers against Eddie Gaedel, the three-foot-seven midget, walking him on four straight high pitches. Yes, it was one of Bill Veeck's shenanigans, much to the distress of Will Harridge, the American League president.)

On the road again, there were times that the routine became monotonous. Finding a hot, talented kid based on questionable tips, stopping at a ballpark to find rest, getting yet another coach's advice took on a feeling of sameness. Names simply became names. Driving the two-lane highways of Kansas, Nebraska, and eastern Colorado bred fatigue, especially on a hot summer afternoon. The heat radiated off the asphalt, creating mirages of cars, trucks, and silos. Then drowsiness crept over you, and within seconds you'd find yourself in a ditch.

Driving from Salina, Kansas, to Hastings, Nebraska, Hughie passed through towns that three decades later the interstates bypassed. Thriving farming towns, they were hubs of commerce for folks thirty to forty miles away. And did they love baseball.

The Hotel Florence in Fairbury, Nebraska, "Your Home When in Fairbury," featured a coffee shop and "modern throughout" facilities. The latter meant each room had its own private bathroom. In

Fairbury Hughie set his attention on three players, Leslie Peden, Joe Murphy, and Isa Glass. Peden was the best of the three. A coach wrote Hugh that he should look at them, as someday they might go all the way.

The month of August meant tournaments and running from Denver to St. Joe to Wichita. The newspapers played it up big to attract crowds in their own towns. Folks loved baseball and flocked to the parks for entertainment. In Wichita well-known teams showed up every year for the national semipro tournament. Hughie watched as many as five games in one day. Some of his favorites included:

the Greeley Jaycees of Greeley, Colorado, an all-star collegiate aggregation

the White Elephants, a Negro Leagues semipro team featuring "Pistol Pete" Albright

the Fort Leavenworth Soldiers, the ranking service team of the nation

the Tractolubers of Lexington, Nebraska, an all-star aggregation, selected from the fast Nebraska Independent League

the Ethiopian Clowns of Miami, Florida, a nationally known, all-black baseball club

Lowry Field, the pick of the seven thousand men from the Army Air Corps School in Denver

For thirty-two consecutive years he attended the tournament, the best one in the country. Any scout worth his salt had to attend.

After the Wichita tournament in 1938, Hughie headed northeast to St. Joe, Missouri, for the annual American Legion All-Star tournament. He had his eye on Pat Curry, a pitcher with some good stuff. After a week in St. Joe he took a break and headed home, only to pack up in a few days to see some more American Legion ball.

Hughie had more territory to cover than any other scout in the country, tens of thousands of square miles with all kinds of leagues. Texas alone had the Lone Star League, the Texas League, and the

Eastern Texas League. Oklahoma had the Sooner State League, and then there was the Western Association, made up of teams from Missouri, Arkansas, Kansas, and Oklahoma. Add the high schools and colleges, and by the outbreak of World War II he knew at least one person in every town with a population of a thousand or more.

Before the war Cleveland usually had ten or more farm clubs at all levels. That was at least three hundred ballplayers that would make the Minor League rosters. But the Indians had to double that number or triple it to find the cream of the crop. With few scouts on the payroll, Hughie plowed ahead determinedly, still combing high school and American Legion ball fields.

What was his record at the end of his first year of scouting? *He didn't sign one player.*

4

Striking Gold in His
Own Backyard

In late March 1939 Hank Iba told Hughie to get to Stillwater in a hurry. The Aggies (now Oklahoma State University) had a hard-throwing right-handed pitcher who was getting some attention from scouts but in a different sport, football. Driving the short distance to Stillwater, Hughie arrived on campus, parked near the ball field, and found Iba.

"Hughie, see that big Indian boy down there in left field throwing the ball? He's a good football player—plays fullback—but he's never played baseball 'til now, and he's a senior. He's got a great arm. In fact, I'll warm him up for you right now. He has a good fastball. He's got pure velocity, and I know some scouts are watching him already. In the five games he's pitched this spring, he has 19, 19, 20, 21, and 22 strikeouts."

Both watched the kid warm up. The ball that he held began to seem less and less like a ball and more and more like a surgeon's scalpel—something used to cut with precision. His fastball had a hop. He intimidated batters. He milked the ball, letting everyone know that the plate was his territory. Any transgressors would be listening to some chin music.

That night Hughie called Slapnicka and told him about Allie Reynolds.

"Keep your eyes on him, Hughie."

The next week Allie pitched a no-hitter. Hughie called Slapnicka.

"We need to sign him. Hank Iba tells me that the Giants are after him to play pro football, and we are going to have to give a little money to sign him."

Slapnicka asked how much.

Hugh replied, "A thousand bucks!"

"We don't have that kind of money," Cy shouted.

"Mr. Slapnicka, I know Major League pitching, and the only pitcher I have seen with a faster ball is Bob Feller. If we don't sign him, he is going to play football."

On a warm spring morning Hughie hopped into his Chevy, prepared to do something momentous—sign Allie Reynolds. Here he was, a twenty-two-year-old kid, signing a twenty-one-year-old Creek Indian for a $1,000 bonus. He headed for the bank, remembering Harry's favorite expression: *Cash is hot!* Borrowing $1,000 from the bank—all in hundred-dollar bills—he paid a visit to Allie's home.

Allie had a wife and a baby. They lived in a small apartment off campus. After some pleasantries, Hughie talked to him and his wife about a baseball career. "Baseball is your game, and you can play the game a lot longer than football and not get beat up. Besides, you want to enjoy playing with your child as he gets older. Here's the offer."

Hughie opened a large envelope and spread the bills out all over the table.

"How much is that?" Allie asked.

"A thousand dollars! It's all yours if you sign now," Hughie replied.

Allie picked up the pen and signed the contract.

The next day Slapnicka sent a wire. "I want to see a $1,000 bonus pitcher immediately. Put that Reynolds on a train to Cleveland." By the no-nonsense wording of the telegram, Hughie knew that Cy was ticked off at him, spending that kind of money on an unproven prospect who had played less than one season of baseball. Hughie took a big chance by not getting his permission, but he knew he had found a pitcher to be in the Big Show with Bob Feller.

He was flush with the feeling of signing a hot prospect as an amateur free agent. He beat football's New York Giants at their own game. While they waited, he had seized the ball and whisked down the field with Allie Reynolds at his side. Nobody was going to beat him in his own backyard.

By mid-June Allie was pitching for the Springfield, Ohio, club. In his first game he won 10-2. In his fourth Minor League season he compiled an 18-7 record with the Class A Wilkes-Barre team and a 1.56 ERA. In 1942 he was called up to the Indians and remained in the big leagues through the 1954 season. In his thirteen years with the Indians and the Yankees, he won 182 and lost 107.

What did Hughie see in Reynolds? Well, he released the ball just at the moment of full extension of his arm. Cy taught him to look for that technique.

Allie knew location—up and down and in and out. He never worried about hitting a batter. Let the batter take care of himself.

What did he have besides a fastball? Nothing, but he was smart. Later he developed a curve and a change of pace. So he had three pitches and spent twelve years in the Majors.

He had the guts of a burglar. Meaning he would throw at you and hit you just like Don Drysdale. That was his temperament. If a pitcher does not have any guts, he cannot pitch. If he gets a lump in his throat, if he worries about hitting a batter, if he has all those doubts, then he cannot pitch. Don't waste your time on him.

Allie spent four years with the Indians and then was traded to the Yankees for Hall of Famer Joe Gordon after the 1946 season. It was a trade that stuck in Hugh's mind in later years, because both the Indians and the Yankees benefited.

"That's the sign of a good trade, when both clubs get what they wanted. No one got suckered," Hughie often remarked in later years.

Mark Twain observed that some experiences are to be avoided, just as a cat would avoid a falling brick. Experience some events in life vicariously and from a distance. One such example was to stay out of trouble with baseball commissioner Kenesaw Mountain Landis.

Commissioner Landis was opposed to signing boys before they graduated from high school. It wasn't long after Hughie began scouting that Landis put in a rule that clubs could not sign a boy until he graduated or his class had graduated. That is still the rule today.

Finding out a kid's date of birth was not a simple matter during the Depression. Thousands of kids born during World War I and the twenties never had a birth certificate issued. Some churches kept baptismal records to verify date of birth, but it was based on parents' recollections. Many children dropped out of school after the eighth grade, so one had to make an educated guess about which year their high school class would graduate.

Hughie got enough advice from his elders about signing boys before they graduated from high school. Of course, there was always some postdating of contracts. If you were caught, you were in trouble. Yes, there were a couple of times that Judge Landis dragged Hughie's butt into his office in Chicago.

Getting off the elevator on the twenty-sixth floor he walked to the judge's office, where the window was painted with just one word in black letters "BASEBALL." Its stark simplicity implied a warning, as if one was guilty and had to prove his innocence.

Opening the door was like walking into purgatory. The judge wasted little time getting to the point. As Landis's eyes darted and his shaggy white hair shook, Hughie felt a freight train coming down the tracks, aimed at him.

"Mr. Alexander, I understand that you have been signing some boys before they graduate from high school and then postdating the contracts." The accusation had only one message—confess his sins. "You know my opposition to this practice. Do you have anything to say?"

Hughie pleaded innocent and wondered silently why anyone would start such rumors. Maybe some of the scouts were jealous of him, a successful upstart. The judge warned him, "If I catch you postdating contracts, Mr. Alexander, I'll throw you out of baseball. You understand me?"

Hughie didn't consider himself a churchgoing man, but the judge sure put the fear of God in his soul. With a tone of solemnity and respect, he replied, "Yes sir, Judge Landis." Decades later, Hughie still saw Landis's eyeballs piercing his brain with that wild shock of white hair glistening. Yeah, he looked like God talking to Moses atop Mt. Sinai.

As Hughie closed the door to Landis's office, he thought if he were caught again, "I'm a goner. If I don't get caught, I'm a great scout." Either way, he knew that he was on Judge Landis's list of people to watch.

Hughie's first brush with Judge Landis sparked a way of thinking about his work. If he thought only about the "thou shall nots," or what could not be done, then he might never consider what could be done. The more effective approach was to know the rules and how they were interpreted. Yes, some clubs would yell and scream, especially when they hadn't thought of the new scheme themselves. That's why the "thou shall not" approach always meant "you'll always be behind." You're always on the defensive, never the offensive. Shrewd minds always think of something else to do, if they know the right questions to ask.

Hughie figured out that small-town beer joints were among the best places to find hot prospects. The late Doug Minor, a White Sox scout, told Hughie that he lived in beer halls because he would get the best tips there. Customers talked straightforwardly, never couched their thoughts in fancy words, and knew the game.

But he reminded himself repeatedly to get to know the people. Don't just walk in and tell them you're a big shot scout and you want some good leads. Be coy and quiet, yet confident. You've got to know the people, face to face. Nothing else counts if they think you are a phony. If you don't try to get people to know you, they'll turn you off. And you can't wait for them to come to you. You've got to go to them and find out what's important in their lives. Start a conversation and get folks to talk about themselves.

Folks also want to know how much you care about them before they care about how much you know. It makes no difference whether you're playing poker or signing a player. You've got to know the territory, as the Music Man said to disbelieving salesmen on a train pulling into River City.

In small towns in the South and the Midwest today, you still have to follow Hughie's advice if you want to get anywhere. According to Hughie, your reputation precedes you, especially when you keep your promises. Don't go around making a lot of promises with no intention of fulfilling them. You may forget them, but others will remember what you forget.

Hughie heard about a high schooler, a Dale Mitchell, who lived near Colony, a nondescript town at the eastern edge of the Oklahoma panhandle. Joe Gore, with whom Hughie played semipro ball in 1934 and '35, called and told him to hightail it out there. Within a couple of days he drove to Paden and checked into the town's hotel.

He asked the clerk, "You wouldn't happen to know a guy by the name of Joe Gore, would you?"

"Sure do," he replied.

"Where can I find him?"

"Right down the street. He works in the beer joint."

Hughie checked into the hotel, unpacked, and walked down the street to the beer joint where Joe tended bar. It was about 3:00 p.m., not a soul inside. Soon they were talking baseball and about his new job.

"So you took my advice to come out to see this kid Dale Mitchell?"

"Sure did," Hughie replied.

"Yeah, he lives about twenty miles from here."

The next day Hughie hopped in his car and headed west. Finally he turned onto a gravel country road to Dale's home. His mother met him at the front screen door. Hughie introduced himself and said why he wanted to meet Dale. In a guarded tone, she told him that Dale was working but he was going to play a game on Sunday at a nearby town.

Hughie went back to town and waited another day. It was worth the wait. On Sunday morning he and Joe (the beer joint was closed) drove over to a town south of Colony to see the boy. Dale Mitchell, a left-handed batter and thrower, greeted them with three triples and a home run. Boy, he could run, but he couldn't throw very well. He had a good eye and rarely struck out. For a kid still in high school to have patience at the plate showed the right stuff.

He was still in high school, but Hughie was determined to sign him. They talked about Dale becoming a pro ballplayer. His eyes glistened. A high school kid who could make money by playing ball beat scratching out a living on the plains of Oklahoma.

"I want to sign him. Don't let anybody get him. I'll be back just before he graduates," Hugh told Joe. Joe promised to "watch over" Dale. A few months later Dale signed for $300. After the war he played with Oklahoma City in the Texas League, batting .337. Not a power hitter, he hit singles and doubles. At the end of the 1946 season the Indians called him up. In eleven games with the Tribe, he hit a whooping .432 (19 for 44).

In his notes, Hugh wrote, "Put him in right field, and hope not many balls are hit out there. Since he can hit and run, we need him." (Despite Hughie's advice, Dale patrolled left field during most of his career.)

Dale had a good eye and struck out only 119 times in his eleven years in the big leagues. From 1946 until 1954 he hit over .300 each year. He played his entire Major League career with the Indians, until they traded him to the Dodgers in late 1956. In 1951 and '52, in 1,021 times at bat he struck out but 25 times. He had a .312 lifetime batting average and a .368 on-base percentage and made only 30 errors in his entire Major League career.

It's ironic that Dale is known among trivia experts as the guy that Don Larsen struck out to get his perfect game in the '56 World Series. Dale always claimed it was a high fastball, but Babe Pinelli, the home plate umpire, hollered a strike. It was the last game in the big leagues for both Dale and Babe.

The Indians fielded some fine teams before the war. In 1940 they finished in second place. And Hughie knew that finding the talent to fill the rosters of the Indians' farm clubs now would make all the difference in the ensuing years.

He "discovered" a lot of boys chasing the dream of playing professionally. Some never discovered it, but they still loved the game. Others became journeymen players, bobbing in and out of big leagues for a "cup of coffee" before finally hanging up their shoes after a few years in the Minors.

Pat Seerey, out of Wilburton, Oklahoma, a fleet outfielder, Hughie found at his high school in Little Rock. The word got around that Seerey was the next home run hitter, despite the number of times he struck out. Hughie signed him immediately. Pat started his rookie year with the Appleton, Wisconsin, club in 1941.

In his three-year stint in the Minor Leagues, Seerey hit over 30 home runs twice and batted over .300. In 1943 the Indians called him up. For four years he played infield for the Indians; being a hustler and having sharp defense became his trademarks. He had a respectable throwing arm and field average, but his batting average hovered around the .225 mark, and he led the league in strikeouts for four years. The year before the Indians won the AL pennant in 1948, he was gone, bags packed for a few more years in the Minors before retiring.

Arkansas was part of his territory. In 1939 Hughie heard about a guy named Williams, a shortstop for the Phillies, living in Greenbrier. His dad ran a baseball school in town. So while Hughie was in Conway scouting a high school player, he made a side trip to Greenbrier to look at the players.

There he spotted Gene Bearden, a left-handed first baseman who was about to be released from his contract. He had flirted around the Minor Leagues and everybody else had given up on him. But he was a battler and was always taking his manager aside asking if he could pitch. He had a nasty slider and a pretty good knuckle ball, which he was always throwing in warm-ups, all season.

The Indians needed a gutsy, smart lefty, so Hughie offered Bearden a tryout. If he could make the cut, he could get him a signing bonus. He took the offer and he made good. After the war he went up to the Indians in 1948. He had a terrific rookie year, posting a 20-7 record for the World Champion Indians.

Change in baseball can be painful. Years of friendships followed by firings and resignations leave a person drifting, especially a twenty-five-year-old who has known only one boss. After Hughie's first five years with the Indians, his mentor and boss Cy Slapnicka resigned from the Indians in 1941.

Hughie had never known anyone else to talk with in the front office. Cy had always checked up on him. "Remember, no golfing. You're paid to go to the ballpark, not the golf course." (Hughie doubted that Cy worried about his playing much golf. There weren't too many one-armed golfers.) "And don't get caught up in a kid's performance. It's the mechanics—the tools of the trade."

5

You Gotta Have a Plan

Bill McKechnie, a Major League manager with a sound knowledge of the game, wrote, "Outside of the major league office, all too little credit is given to the baseball scout, who, today, roams the country from one end to the other, constantly on the lookout for 'major-league timber.'

"He is the eyes of baseball. Without him major-league ball would soon become minor-league ball. Not only does the scout check carefully on the mechanical ability of every potential candidate, but when his report goes in to the front office you can be sure that it contains a complete record of every player's moral character, his physical ability, his disposition, and many other qualifications to which the average fan gives all too little thought."

Although Hughie probably never read McKechnie's comments about scouts, he certainly practiced them. He was going to be the best scout, a one-armed David maneuvering around the Goliaths of the baseball world. When he decided to go after a kid, he was going to sign him. And he wanted other scouts to know that he signed only future Major Leaguers. It was just expected. He was determined to leave a good set of fingerprints on every deal he made.

It was midsummer 1941 in a ballpark in Pueblo, Colorado. Hughie never forgot the chance meeting. Branch Rickey apparently had heard about him and recognized him in the park. Rickey sent word that he wanted Hughie to come up to talk with him about a Minor League deal.

Rickey's signature bow tie and bushy eyebrows left no one to wonder who he was. His dress did not convey any humble beginnings in small-town Ohio. His highly polished shoes glistened even in the shade of the stadium. A neatly cornered handkerchief tucked carefully in his breast pocket and tightly creased slacks conveyed an image of a man in control of his destiny. Conspicuous success was written all over his countenance.

"I've heard a lot about you, young man. Even some old scouts think you have the makings of good future in baseball. You're smart, always thinking about another deal to make," he began.

"Son," he said, "let me give you a little advice. When you get on the fence with a ballplayer, walk away, walk away from him. You'll make a mistake if you don't."

"Boy, was he right. He was one of the masters of finding talented ballplayers in the whole history of the game," Hughie reflected on the advice, decades later.

Following Rickey's advice paid big dividends, because he just didn't make mistakes, at least in the mind of a scout in his midtwenties.

Rickey gave Hughie some good advice on spotting effective pitchers that later appeared in Rickey's *Little Blue Book*. In his opinion, good pitching produces delusions by making a batter misjudge a ball. The game would be violated if a pitcher did not practice becoming proficient in deception, whether the pitch was a curve, a change of pace, or a rising fastball.

He also made an important distinction between control and location. When a pitcher throws a slider, down and out, that is a great pitch. It may be called a ball, but the pitcher had location, direction, and control. To the casual fan, it was a bad pitch. Better that kind of pitch than a curve ball over the plate that goes for a home run. Yes, the pitcher had control, but poor location and direction. Likely the ball landed in the bleachers in far left field, not in the catcher's mitt.

As the *Little Blue Book* further explained, "A pitcher also had to become an effective fielder. That quality Rickey found in Don Newcombe who moved his feet properly to go after a bunt or slow roller. He kept his balance after delivering the ball, ready to pounce on any ball in his direction."

Rickey, the founder of the farm system, as general manager of the Cardinals from 1926 to 1942 took a Major League club that had floundered for years, a club with little money, and built it within a few years into a contender. Although he was fired as manager of the Cardinals in 1925, he found his niche in the front office as general manager. The next year his Cardinals, under new manager Rogers Hornsby, won the NL pennant and went on to upset the Bronx Bombers in the World Series.

Rickey told his scouts to sign players. Go for quantity instead of quality. If other teams' scouts signed three players, he would sign ten or twelve. The odds were in his favor. The cream comes to the top, and then he used a lot of the other players for trading.

As a lawyer, Rickey thought about other ways to control the flow and development of young players. Why not own entire leagues? By 1938 the Cardinals backed entire leagues, such as Arkansas-Missouri and the Nebraska State Leagues. Let the good players wear the Cardinal uniform. Sell the others for a handsome profit. Judge Landis put a stop to these efforts; he called owning entire Minor Leagues a threat to the integrity of the game and ordered the release of seventy-four Cardinal farmhands.

Never docile, Rickey rebuilt his empire. Hughie knew about Rickey's aggressiveness and reputation as one never to back down, even if it meant losing a job. Now, at a ballpark in his fourth year of scouting, he got raw, candid advice about planning from the business guru of baseball.

Every kid who ever played on at least one sandlot team heard the coach holler, "Anticipate! Know what you're going to do with the ball if it comes your way! You gotta think!" For Hughie, planning and anticipating came together after those few conversations with Rickey. As a kid he saw a lot of ranchers break horses in a pen. When the rancher got into the pen, he used a soft, determined approach, but always with a wary eye. You gotta anticipate what one thousand pounds of unbridled fury can do in a heartbeat, or you don't last long.

Rickey did not stop planning after setting up the farm system. He had another plan, as outlined in *Branch Rickey's Little Blue Book*: "The system offered a selection of better players. We knew our own material; we had followed it for several years. We brought it along to each level. We controlled the instruction and discipline and we had a much better idea of a player's major-league ability." Every Minor League manager was expected to follow a strict regimen of defensive routines, such as practicing relays from an outfielder to an infielder with men on the bases and bases empty or overthrowing an infielder. Rickey outlined different double play routines with the orders to practice them every day. Pick-off plays, back-ups, and covering the bases on bunts made up other drills.

He expected players to learn these fundamentals in the Minor Leagues, not in the Majors. With a farm club system, he demanded a "sticking to the fundamentals." Fans in the big leagues do not come to the park to watch players learn the game by screwing up. He demanded his players do their practicing elsewhere.

Rickey maintained that the biggest mistake a scout makes is not sorting out all the information in evaluating players. He felt that scrambled written observations led to confused thinking. Furthermore, he cautioned Hughie about getting involved with too many trades at one time, because you forget what you tell each club. That will really foul you up. If you're dealing with two or three clubs, you're playing both ends against the middle. The first thing you know, you've got three clubs that want to make a trade for the same players. Now what are you going to do?

Hughie loved to compete with the big guys, the veterans of the scouting fraternity. Maybe that attitude singled him out in Rickey's mind from any of the other young scouts.

Rickey taught Hughie to know your market and earn enough authority to make a quick signing. If the front office is uncertain about a player, don't ask for permission to sign unless you are certain you will get the answer you want. Hughie took a lot of chances while lesser scouts played their cards conservatively.

If Rickey peppered Hughie about making plans, Cy Slapnicka taught him about developing contacts. "He was a helluva scout," Hughie observed about Cy.

Continuously, Cy harped on making contacts. "Wherever you go, be sure you make a contact. Talk to the baseball coach of whatever town you're in. And get acquainted with these people. Think of every one of them as a friend who will help you someday.

"So whenever you hear about a player in Mississippi, you'll say, 'I know the coach down there. I met them.' Pick up the phone and call the coach and say, 'Do you have a ballplayer by such-and-such a name. What do you think about him?'

He might say he's good or might say no way. And if he says no, it saves you a hell of a trip. You trust his advice, because you know him."

Interestingly, some of Hughie's best contacts were from other scouts and general managers from the other clubs. Call it inside information, but they were always looking for something in return. He knew that they would come around in a not too subtle manner and say, "You like that guy?"

"Yeah, I like him," Hughie might reply.

He didn't share too much information. He just wasn't going to do it. Every scout he broke in heard him say, "Don't give up your information. You worked like hell to get it, so dammit, keep it to yourself. Don't give it away, and don't trade it away."

A lot of scouts used to give away information, usually beginning with "I'll trade you so-and-so, if you reciprocate." Hugh learned early not to play that game except when it was to his advantage.

"Ain't no way I'm going to join that crowd," Hughie remarked.

And he used to tell his scouts in later years that if he caught them exchanging information, he'd fire their "ass so fast they won't know what's going on."

Any job can become routine after a couple of years, and scouting is no exception. Someone asked Hughie if there was a routine to finding talent. In scouting, there is no beginning, middle, or ending. Sometimes you begin in the middle and then begin all over again. Music is like that. Some verses you sing over and over again to learn to love the music. Scouting is like that.

His challenge was always to mine the talent. It's hard to do when the club's broke or when nobody values what you do. What is equally hard or more difficult to do is to keep your team performing at a championship level year after year. Sheer determination is not an answer. Neither is just spending money on ballplayers. What is important is spending it wisely and with a plan.

By 1941 Hugh's reputation got around the circuit. Scouts, spotting him in towns, immediately asked, "Who is Hughie looking at?" That's the way he wanted it. Whenever he walked into a ballpark or hotel lobby, he got people thinking, "What's Hughie up to? Who's he scouting?"

Hughie had to play a few tricks, some "smoke and mirrors" to take them off the trail, that he picked up from carnies in earlier years. Sometimes he zigzagged around the back alleys or talked to a player he had no real interest in so that they would not find it easy to know his real reason for coming to town. Other times Hughie just arrived in a town for no reason other than to get the scouts talking. That was a good way to find out quickly who were the smart ones and the dumb ones. Maybe they just wanted to be around him, thinking that something might rub off.

In the late fifties Hughie spotted one scout constantly peeking over his shoulder, trying to read his notes. Finally, Hughie figured a good way to teach him a lesson was to put some fictitious notes on his dashboard about a hot prospect in a town about 150 miles away.

No mistake, the scout took the bait. He spotted the notes about Hughie's new "discovery." Dammit, he was mad when he showed up at the ballpark the next day. After driving three hundred miles for a nonexistent player, he knew that all the other scouts thought him as a sucker. Every profession has a few guys like him.

"If you want to get a soldier, you have to go through Mom, and moms want to know what kind of future their children will have when they leave the army," said Lt. Col. Jeff Sterling, the army's architect of the 2011 "Buy All You Can Buy" recruiting campaign.

Slapnicka's advice to Hughie in 1938 preceded the military's efforts in 2011. The message endures: "Mama knows best." If a scout wants to sign top talent from the high school diamond, he needs to know their mamas. He talks to a mom and learns what she wants for her son. That begins with an invitation to dinner. There you can watch Mom and her boy talk to one another and the kinds of questions and advice she gives. If she is suffocating her son with all kinds of concern, it raises a red flag.

Hughie always was searching for a way to find a competitive advantage over those in the same business. Harry had taught him to be aggressive, but with a smile on his face. He learned people's names and their birthdays, what they like and don't like. Hughie learned ways to begin a conversation. What's a good way to begin a conversation with a stranger? Get him to talk about himself.

Festina lente, "make haste slowly." Keep looking with a sharp eye. Just keep moving along. Remember the S.W. Rule: Some Will, Some Won't, and So What? (Who's Next?) Baseball became Hugh's identity. Baseball was who he was, even if he had only one hand. He still had two eyes and two ears.

6

Scouting in Wartime

At the end of the 1941 season Hughie got a taste of baseball's painful side. Ossie Vitt, the Indians' manager, was fired, replaced by Roger Peckinpaugh, and Cy Slapnicka, Hughie's mentor, resigned. Cy had been with the club since 1923 as a scout and vice president. It was Hughie's first lesson that it was easier to fire a manager and front office personnel than to make wholesale changes in the dugout.

Two months later the Japanese Empire bombed Pearl Harbor. America was at war in Europe and in the Far East. Like other sports, baseball quickly faded into the background. A number of players enlisted, like Bob Feller, who joined the navy. Others were drafted within months. Hughie, like other baseball people, thought that baseball would not be played, but no one really knew.

Weeks later, in early January 1942, Judge Landis and the owners considered canceling the Major League Baseball season. Baseball club rosters rapidly shrunk. Gas and car tires were rationed, and the railroads were used to transport troops to bases across the nation. Travel for leisure and entertainment took a back seat. To many fans and followers, this was not the time to play baseball.

The next month President Roosevelt wrote a letter to Landis asking him to let the game continue. It was good for the nation's morale. Civilian workers needed a diversion, and nothing was better than the national pastime.

The scouts working for Cleveland were issued these orders: "Do whatever you can, but traveling will be severely restricted." (Cleveland had only two or three scouts in 1941, and no more would be hired during the war.) Hughie couldn't travel much. It didn't matter anyway, because there were no ballplayers left. They were all drafted. Over five hundred ballplayers eventually served in the armed services during the war. The immediate policy question clubs faced: Should players above and below the military draft age be allowed to play? The owners and commissioner quickly decided to let them play. Otherwise, the game would be shut down.

Altogether, twenty Cleveland players served in the armed forces, including Bob Feller, Tom Ferrick, Harry Eisenstat, Bob Lemon, Eddie Robinson, Ken Keltner, Jim Hegan, Hank Edwards, and Gene Woodling.

In the summer of 1942 the Service All-Stars of Cleveland formed a ball club that included Vinnie Smith, Don Padgett, Ernie Andres, Herm Fishman, Fred Schaffer, Frankie Pytlak, Russ Meers, Johnny Lucadello, Don Dunker, O. V. Mulkey, Fred Hutchinson, Sam Chapman, Bob Feller, George Earnshaw, Mickey Cochrane, Hank Gowdy, Joe Grace, Cecil Travis, Mickey Harris, John Rigney, Ken Silvestri, Pat Mullin, Johnny Sturm, Sam Harshaney, Chet Hajduk, Bob Peterson, John Grodzicki, Mush Esler, Benny McCoy, Emmett Mueller, and Morris Arnovich.

With the wartime travel restrictions, Hughie visited ballparks in Dallas, Fort Worth, and Beaumont infrequently because of gas and tire rationing. Tulsa and Oklahoma City, near his home, offered better choices to look at a few guys. He just did the best he could, as his hands were tied. At least he kept his job.

He spent a lot of time traveling on buses and trains. Usually civilians stood in the aisle the entire trip, allowing women, children, and soldiers to sit. If there was no train or bus, he hitchhiked a ride to the next town. Gas stamps remained hard to get. The most he could get was four gallons at a time with one ration stamp. But he learned a little trick of the trade with T stamps. *T* stood for truck, and each truck could get five gallons of gas with a T stamp.

In 1943 a buddy he worked with in the oil drilling business owned a fleet of trucks, and the government sent him a lot of T stamps. One day Hughie was complaining about not having enough stamps to go anywhere. His buddy pulled Hughie inside his office, shut the door, pulled out a desk drawer, and whispered, "I got a drawer full of T stamps I never use." He gave Hughie a handful of them but warned him, "Don't tell the guy at the pump that you want ten gallons. Just say, 'eight gallons.' After you get the gas, hand him the T stamps and drive off."

Pulling up to a gas station, Hughie nonchalantly asked the attendant for eight gallons of gas. After he pumped the gas, Hughie gave him two T stamps.

"Hey, I can't take those stamps. Those are for trucks. That's against the law."

"Well, siphon it out!" Hughie yelled as he jumped into his car and sped off.

"Don't you ever come back to my station, you son of a bitch!" The words faded in the distance as Hughie drove off to an army base to watch a tournament.

Creature comforts didn't exist for the civilian traveler, not that GIs had it any easier. Most towns had small, clapboard hotels with ten to twelve rooms and a bathroom at the end of hallway. A gloomy lobby with a couple of overstuffed chairs, a beat-up coffee table, and a lamp with a sixty-watt bulb greeted the tired motorist at the end of the day.

Hotel owners needed lessons in cockroach and grasshopper extermination. Every room Hughie slept in had a Depression-era look. The grimy wallpaper with a hint of a floral design was probably cleaned five years ago. A light hung from the ceiling in the center of the room. To get some fresh air, one raised the window but checked first to see if there were any holes in screens. June bugs, flies, and mosquitoes loved the sight of a lightbulb, as their dinner hour arrived with dusk.

To get some entertainment, one turned on the radio and inevitably got the late-night station out of Del Rio, Texas, with some preacher praying for everybody's sins. Sleeping in a sticky, hot hotel room swatting bugs and other varmints didn't give one much time to think about his sins.

In early 1942 the Texas League officials and club owners decided to stop playing ball until the war's end. Several other Minor Leagues suspended playing, but the players still belonged to the clubs. Only by getting permission from the club that owned him could a player play.

Spring training was also affected. In 1943, to free up train transportation for military personnel, Judge Landis ruled that no club could go south of the Ohio or Potomac Rivers nor west of the Mississippi (with the exception of the St. Louis Browns and Cardinals). Most clubs stayed close to home. The Indians held spring training outdoors in freezing weather and in nearby high school gyms.

Hughie signed only a couple of players during the war. They couldn't play well, but there were a few good semipro players trying to catch a scout's eye. Some of the big league clubs signed them for a couple hundred dollars and let them play a little if someone was injured. Most of time they just sat on the bench, hoping for just one chance to show their stuff.

Finally Hughie decided to go around to the army camps (Texas, Louisiana, and Oklahoma had several army installations) to watch baseball. The rumor going around the scouting circuit that at least he could see good baseball. Maybe he'd see somebody he knew and stick around for a couple of days.

"Let me know if you see anybody. Remember your friend Hughie," he said as he smiled and waved a hello. Everybody knew that the "Old Redhead" was on the base.

Damn, he was struggling. His feet hurt from doing a lot of walking in worn-out shoes. A new pair of shoes would bring instant relief but, like gasoline and tires, they were rationed. When the soles wore out, people cut pieces of cardboard and inserted them into the shoes for at least a few hours of comfort.

Finally, he spotted a former ballplayer who worked in the PX. "I could really use a new pair of shoes." Hughie didn't try to hide what he needed.

"What size?" the private replied.

"Size ten."

The next day Hughie picked up a pair of army boots. "How much?" Hughie asked.

"Two bucks," whispered the private.

At least he didn't have another case of tired feet for a few months. Now he could keep trying to stay in touch with some of the ballplayers and find out when they were getting out of the service, especially when late 1944 and early 1945 rolled around. He'd be there at the army gate, just waiting with a contract and a pen, a promise made repeatedly.

He found a catcher out of Fort Bliss in El Paso. Hughie was sitting right there when he got discharged. A lot of other army and flyboys singled him out, wanting to get signed immediately after discharge.

"Hey, Hughie, don't forget me when I'm discharged next September."

"You tell me where you're going to be and I'll be there. I'll come get ya," Hughie yelled, then flashed a big Okie grin.

Ballplayers stationed on the army bases got a little better deal than the other GIs. They played a lot of ball and didn't have canteen or latrine duty. The better ones would go to the biggest tournament in the whole country, always held on an army base in Arkansas. San Antonio hosted the army air corps tournament for the flyboys.

In early 1943 he heard about some good players at Randolph Army Air Corps Base in San Antonio. A colonel ran the program. He was always recruiting players and always pumping Hughie for names of guys from his contacts at other bases. He took Hughie aside: "I want some good players. You tell me about some damn good prospects at other bases. Just call me on the phone and leave word, if you don't mind. You just get me his name. I'll get him. I got that much pull." Damn if he didn't. He won the national championships five years in a row for his army air corps base. So Hughie hooked up with the colonel to begin scouting for him on the side, because he knew the colonel would give him some hot tips after the war. It was a good trade: Hughie's advice now for getting inside the base later, before any other scouts showed up.

While staying around the military bases let Hughie see a lot of games, there was a catch; the army and air corps had some good players, but no one could sign them. Wait until the day of their discharge. The only thing a scout could do was sit and wait.

By the end of the war the Major League clubs still had few scouts. Hughie thought he had the world by the tail. He had watched all those boys in Texas, Arkansas, Oklahoma, and Louisiana. Now they were getting out of the service in droves.

His good contacts began to pay off. A fellow by the name of Eddie (Hughie had met him a few years earlier when he signed up with the Cardinal organization) was managing in Johnson City, Tennessee. He called Hughie: "Hey, son, I need some help. I need some ballplayers."

"Okay, I'll meet with you. Come on down and we'll talk," Hughie answered. Of course they became great friends. They got some good prospects for each other, although Hughie never let the Cleveland front office know about his side jobs.

Well, a good thing can't last too long. With Hughie signing a lot of players just getting out of the service, the word got around to other club officials, including Branch Rickey, now with the Brooklyn Dodgers. A baseball war broke out. Soon Rickey got a rule setting a cap for signing players. Well, at least Hughie got what he wanted for a few months after V-J Day.

The veterans quickly filled the rosters they had vacated a few years earlier. Minor Leagues thrived, too, and by the late forties there were fifty-nine leagues and more than 460 teams, not including the semipros. Along with the Negro Leagues, they provided the glue that held communities and small towns together.

Hugh picked up the same routine he had before the war, hitting the roads to find the raw talent. As Leonard Koppett wrote in *The Thinking Fan's Guide to Baseball*, "It all began in the bushes. That's where you found players. That's where you saw them play."

Hughie spent a lot of time at home in Seminole. He married a hometown girl, Thelma, and had a daughter named Pat. They spent a lot of time with his brother Doc and sister Edith, playing cards all night long or heading to a local beer joint to play shuffleboard. During and after the war, every beer joint and pool hall had a shuffleboard table. People played hour after hour, drinking beer, eating hamburgers, and smoking cigarettes.

One night Hughie suggested they go to a club to play shuffleboard. When they arrived, two men already had a game going on. So they waited and waited for the men to finish. Finally the two men sat down. Doc and Hughie set up to play when the two men came back and said they wanted to play.

Doc told them he and his brother were going to play, and one of the men said, "The hell you are. We were here first."

Hughie told them to go back and sit down. The men said they didn't think they would, and about that time one of them looked down at Hughie's left arm and said, "Oh, I'm sorry. I didn't know you were handicapped."

Thelma got up and hurriedly went to the car, because she knew what was going to happen. Sure enough, Hughie got up and hit the guy, knocking him all the way to the front door, and then continued hitting him.

Edith saw the waitress pick up the phone to call the police. Edith told her to tell them to hurry. They left before the police arrived.

Nobody was ever to call Hughie "handicapped." In his mind it was profanity.

7

After the War, the Show Goes On

World War II was over. GIs came home ready to live a life of normalcy after twelve years of the Great Depression and four years of war. In late 1945 fans waited with heightened anticipation for the new baseball season to begin.

Hall of Famers like Bob Feller, Hank Greenberg, and Joe DiMaggio rejoined their Major League clubs within weeks. The Steve Souchocks, the Hank Bauers, the Cliff Mapeses, and the Eddie Stewarts took off their military uniforms and put on their baseball outfits to play in the Minors, fighting their way up to the Big Show. The journeymen players had to compete with top high school and American Legion kids for a place on club rosters. Fans flocked to the parks wanting to see better players than those who had populated club rosters during the war. Good but untried prospects got a small bonus.

The Indians' front office in Cleveland continued to change personnel. More guys Hughie grew up with during the past ten years had left. When Slapnicka took a scouting job with the St. Louis Browns in 1942 he asked Hughie to come with him, but Hughie said no thanks. He saw nothing in the Browns except failure and no money.

That same year the Indians promoted Lou Boudreau, making him, at age twenty-four, the youngest player-manager in Major League history. Roger Peckinpaugh moved up to the general manager position with the club the same year.

In 1946 Bill Veeck, only thirty years old, got some businessmen to form a syndicate to buy the Indians. With a flair only a carnie could have (Veeck was long known as the P. T. Barnum of baseball), he put in a wholesale array of marketing strategies to get fans into the ballpark. Ladies' Day, his father's creation in Chicago in the twenties, appeared again on Saturday afternoon games. Then he pulled off another marketing trick. He offered all Cleveland radio stations free rights to broadcast the games. Within weeks he had four stations covering the Indians. The year before not one radio station broadcast the games. Veeck just knew how to market anything. He got people to come to the park. Boy, he loved novelties.

The cavernous Cleveland Municipal Stadium, built to house the Olympics in 1932 (Los Angeles got the bid), and League Park II, a 1910 relic, continued to split the home schedule for the Indians. Municipal Stadium hosted the Sunday and holiday games. No other Major League club endured fifteen years playing home games in two different parks.

Veeck turned the club around with Bob Feller, a war hero. He was intent on building a winner. Just at the end of the '46 season he announced a headline-grabbing trade. Allie Reynolds, the first player Hughie signed, was shipped off to the Yankees. The Indians got Joe Gordon to be their new second baseman.

Reynolds, thirty-one, had an 11-15 record, to be only his second and last losing season in the Majors. Gordon, also thirty-one, hit .210 for the Yankees. Hughie hated to see Reynolds leave the Indians, but he knew that one bad season would not break Allie's spirit and determination. As Rickey had reminded him a few years earlier about trades: if both teams profit by a trade, everyone is a winner and it sends a clear message to other teams that trading with the Indians is good business.

Gordon and Lou Boudreau built a solid double play combination leading to a 1948 pennant and World Series championship, the first for Cleveland since 1920. Reynolds teamed with Vic Raschi, Joe Page, and Eddie Lopat to win pennants and World Series championships for the Yankees.

In 1951 Reynolds became the first AL pitcher to hurl two no-hitters in one season. That same year he won the Hickok Belt as the top professional athlete of the year. Gordon was posthumously inducted into the Baseball Hall of Fame in 2009.

The Boudreau-Gordon double play combination was a key to the Indians' winning the pennant, behind the pitching corps of Bob Feller, Bob Lemon, and Steve Gromek. However, Boudreau, the player-manager, held rookie Gene Bearden as his trump card. Hughie, having signed Bearden and Dale Mitchell, breathed a deep feeling of pride. His players made a difference. Bearden's 2.43 ERA led the league, along with six shutouts among his twenty wins.

The Indians tied the Red Sox for the pennant on the final day of the regular season and then traveled to Fenway Park for one playoff game. Bearden was Boudreau's choice for pitcher, although he had only one day's rest. Baseball experts scoffed at a left-handed knuckleballer pitching in Fenway Park. Bearden upheld Boudreau's decision by besting the Red Sox 8–3 to go to the World Series against the Braves.

Bearden's knuckle ball dazzled the Braves' batters. Bearden won one game, a five-hit shutout in the third game of the World Series. In just ten days he pitched four complete games. In the sixth and final game he relieved Bob Lemon in the eighth inning to get the final five outs and a save. The Indians had won their first World Series title since 1920.

Over 2.6 million fans watched the Indians, then a Major League record. "Promotion plus a winning record breaks attendance records," opined "Sportshirt" Bill Veeck.

It was a historic team, featuring seven future Hall of Famers: Bob Feller, Bob Lemon, Joe Gordon, Lou Boudreau, Larry Doby, and the forty-two-year-old rookie Satchel Paige. Veeck, the seventh inductee, rounded out a team stamped as a "baseball original." Hughie got his first World Series ring. He began a streak that lasted his entire career—working for a winner.

A strong pitching corps of Feller, Lemon, Early Wynn, and Mike Garcia with fine hitting by Luke Easter, Al Rosen, and Larry Doby kept the Indians in contention for several years.

To control the number of players signed by a club and to reduce player salaries, the owners set up a bonus rule in 1947. An amateur player receiving a signing bonus of more than $4,000 could not be optioned out. The club that signed him had to keep him or subject him to a draft-waiver system. However, the rule was hard to enforce and by 1950 it was repealed. Under-the-table agreements among the clubs made the rule unenforceable. Big gambling on untried talent continued, as rosters had to be filled in the Minor Leagues.

Back home in Oklahoma, Hughie continued to face his perennial nemeses, the Yankees and the Cardinals. He couldn't compete with them in popularity or money. They owned the Great Plains. All the kids ever heard about were the Yankees and the Cardinals. Both clubs had large farm club systems and rich legacies. Whenever hot prospects talked about baseball, the first words out of their mouths were "New York" and "St. Louis." Kids had visions only of pinstripes and red birds dancing in their heads.

Hughie, ever the gamer, had to come up with a plan. The Goliaths of Major League Baseball were not about to run him out of his territory. When you can't compete with someone with bigger money bags, you've got to think like a politician. How can you persuade someone that you don't think needs persuading? First, you find out what makes the person tick. What is it that appeals to his better self, always remembering all the favors you did for him? Then you keep your promises, not that you should ever make many.

Hughie focused on where a ballplayer could go with his team. A kid had a chance to play ball even if the money was less. The message: forget the big boys. Do you want to play *now*? Or do you want to sit on a bench hoping your time will come with the Yankees or the Cardinals? Chances are that even if you made it to New York or St. Louis, you wouldn't play much or you would get traded.

He had his hands full convincing kids to stick with him. He had to use his connections. The American Legion, high school, and JUCO coaches became his spokesmen, so when he met with a kid, the first words from his lips were, "Hey, I've heard of you before." Slapnicka was right about making contacts.

When these rising stars knew about the possibility of making it, Hughie appealed to what was best in them—if they put heart and talent together, they could make it to the Big Show.

It was about 1949 when he heard about a kid out of Commerce, just a short hop northeast of Seminole, who was being chased by everyone. The kid, a switch-hitting shortstop, could hit with power. Hughie penciled his name, *Mickey Mantle*, in his pocket book.

Later he scouted the "talked-about" kid for a friend at a game in Joplin, Missouri. "No prospect," he wrote. The boy struck out fourteen times in the last week. What Hughie omitted was that the boy hit eight home runs.

He put Joplin in his travel book. "Got to see him again!" But the Yankees beat him by a day. They signed Mickey right under Hughie's nose and in his own backyard.

Meanwhile, rumblings of change became more evident, not only in baseball but also in America. Hughie didn't pay much attention, as the Indians had a lot of Minor League rosters to fill. The big news, however, was integration. Jackie Robinson in Brooklyn and Larry Doby in Cleveland, within three months of each other in 1947, created headlines by joining their Major League teams.

8

Watch, but Don't Pick

When Hughie began scouting in 1938, there was no such thing as signing a black player. It was taboo. It was against the unwritten and unspoken rules in Major League Baseball, although Judge Landis remarked that there was no rule prohibiting black players from playing. Black players had their league, white players, theirs. That was the way things were.

Hughie admitted he felt handicapped, but occasionally he watched black players on barnstorming teams and in the Negro Leagues. Whenever he was in Kansas City or Chicago he stopped to see the Monarchs and American Giants play. He saw some great players but never thought about signing any of them. It never went through his mind, because it was against the unspoken and unwritten rule.

In later years someone asked him who made the rule. He replied, "I don't know, and I didn't know who made the rule. It was just like a lot of Jim Crow attitudes."

The Negro League clubs gave their home crowds both baseball and great entertainment. They had dances on the field, followed by pepper ball. When the House of David arrived in town with their signature black beards, the crowds rallied to the occasion with cheering and applause.

In those days the black communities rallied behind their teams. On opening day, parades featuring the local high school bands marched down the street followed by the players and their wives, coaches, and staff, all piled into convertibles, waving to the crowds. Fans dressed in their best finery. Men wore dress hats, suits, and ties, and women donned brightly colored dresses and hats, highlighted with white gloves and purses.

Black communities in many of these cities had vibrant businesses. Banks, small insurance companies, a newspaper, beauty shops, and nightclubs dotted the neighborhoods. These small businesses served as anchors, giving stability and economic vitality.

In Kansas City the area around Eighteenth and Vine bustled with activity day and night. Duke Ellington, Charlie Parker, and Louis Armstrong lit up the town. People danced in the streets as music blared over a loudspeaker. Jazz, pretty women, and baseball—a winning combination. That's why Negro ballplayers loved Kansas City, with the ballpark just a half mile away.

Only after World War II did the rumor pop up that Branch Rickey was going to sign a player from the Negro Leagues. But no one paid much attention to it.

The rumors became more pronounced in late 1946 about a black player coming to the Majors. Occasionally Hughie asked himself about the potential repercussions. Most of them were bad, real bad, real B-A-D. Growing up in a small town in Oklahoma, Hughie lived in a highly segregated world, not unlike blacks and whites elsewhere in America. If any blacks lived nearby, they and whites played on separate teams and in different ballparks. That arrangement was just the way the world was. Any change invited problems, even fighting, and baseball would not be immune from violence in the grandstand or on the field.

Finally, after nearly fifty years, the Minor Leagues opened its doors to black players. Rickey signed Jackie Robinson in 1945, sending him to Montreal, a farm club of the Dodgers. Al Campanis and Clyde Sukeforth worked with Robinson before bringing him up to the Dodgers in 1947.

When Jackie did come up, he couldn't stay in a white hotel. Racial slurs were thrown at him, and oftentimes he simply turned the other cheek. As Rickey wrote in his *Little Blue Book*, "Turning the other cheek means not receiving the second blow. It means cutting the chains of the inevitable wrongs at the first link. Your adversary is ready for anything but this."

What a lot of people forget is that Bill Veeck brought up Larry Doby within three months of Robinson. Doby was playing with the Newark Eagles when the deal was made. Veeck bought his contract for $10,000, plus another $10,000 if he made the Indians.

Observed Hughie, "I'm not running anybody down, but Doby was the better player, if you graded them on the field. He had a lot of home runs. He was one of the few players, maybe the second or third one, to hit a ball out of the old Senators' ballpark."

When Doby put on the Cleveland uniform in July 1947, he benefited from Robinson's breaking the barrier. Most baseball fans figured that Robinson would be the only black man to play, at least that year. They didn't know Bill Veeck. The Cleveland fans treated Doby well. Hughie didn't hear or remember very many incidents of trouble erupting between him and the fans compared to what hit Robinson. It was tough on Doby when he had to stay in a black hotel and eat in a black restaurant. He became belligerent because he thought he should be able to stay in the white hotel and eat in the white restaurant, but he didn't make it a big issue.

About Doby, little has been written. People in the Cleveland organization never heard about any special kind of coaching given to him before or even after he came up. He didn't need any, because he was a self-made man, a natural athlete.

In the late spring of 1947 Hughie headed back to the high school and college ballparks, now in his ninth year of scouting. One of the first tips he got was to look at a football player, an All-American at an all-black school in Baton Rouge.

"He was a helluva outfielder. He could really play baseball," observed Hughie as he tried to sign him up, but the kid just wouldn't sign. (Hughie did not recall his name.) He said, "Mr. Alexander, I love baseball, but I can go right into the big leagues in football and make big money real quick. If I sign with you, I gotta go to the Miami league and all that. I don't want to spend four or five years in the Minors. That's too long."

Although more black players were signed in the early fifties, there was still no great burning desire to scout black players. Some people, including scouts, were still apprehensive about whether they ought to put black players in the big leagues, because the fans might stay away from the park. Fans might boycott and tell the owners to hell with you. It was a slow process, taking another twelve years for all clubs to become integrated.

At the same time some scouts set their eyes on the Caribbean and Central America, especially in the Dominican Republic, Cuba, Mexico, and Panama. A lot of black players adopted Hispanic names and became Cubans or Panamanians, not black. Labels made a difference.

Hughie remembered a college football coach in the Deep South who didn't recruit black players. He didn't believe in them until he saw a black high school kid take the ball at the 5-yard line and return it 95 yards for a touchdown. The coach jumped up and down, shouting, "Look at that Indian run!" The coach changed his mind and was converted in ten seconds as the kid raced to the goal line.

When Hughie signed Allie Reynolds, there was no problem with his being a Creek Indian. Besides, the Creeks were well-to-do people. Allie's father was a minister and had an education. However, the club was careful about signing Indian ballplayers, believing that they became alcoholics easily.

Integration was a long process, slowed not only by clubs wondering about the fans' reactions but also by some veteran scouts who pulled out the race card when trying to sign a white boy. Whispering to a boy's parents, a scout would say, "You wouldn't want your boy sleeping in the same room with a n———. Now, if he signed with the Dodgers (or Indians or Giants), that might happen." The psychology of fear was pumped through many kids' and parents' minds with no quick remedy. Most parents didn't want any part of that situation.

After Hughie took a scouting job with the White Sox in 1953, he wanted the team to sign Ernie Banks, but Frank Lane, the general manager, turned him down. He thought that Banks didn't field well enough, although he sure could hit.

Hughie knew Buck O'Neil, manager of the Kansas City Monarchs. Buck had called him to talk about Banks. "You got to take a look at him, because we've had a few people come to see him already."

Hughie called Lane, who told him to go to Kansas City. The Monarchs were playing in Denver, but Hugh watched Banks in several games upon the Monarchs' return to Kansas City and then called Lane.

"This boy can really hit. His arm is average. He is not a real good shortstop either, but he can hit, and somewhere along the line we can find a place for him to play." Lane wanted a letter about him, so Hughie wrote over a page telling Lane why the White Sox should sign him. But Lane's mind was on other matters, mainly trading players.

Finally, Lane called asking about Banks. "I'll scout him this Sunday at the Negro League All-Star game at Comiskey Park," he told Hughie.

On Monday Lane called back. "I don't like him."

"What do you mean, you don't like him?" Hughie asked.

"He made a couple of errors," Lane quickly replied.

"Well," Hughie said, "a lot of guys do that. We're going to make a hell of a mistake, Frankie, if we don't take this guy. He is going to hit a bunch of home runs."

"Here's what I want you to do," Lane insisted. "I want you to call Tom Baird [owner of the Monarchs], and I want you to offer him $7,500 for him. I think he has already been offered $25,000 or $30,000, and he's damn sure not going to take $7,500. I want you to call him and tell him."

So Hughie had to call Baird, which was embarrassing. "Tom, this is not me talking, but Lane wants to buy Banks for $9,000, maybe $10,000," Hughie began the conversation.

Baird said, "Hell, no. I can't do that."

"I don't blame you," Hughie answered.

About a week later the Cubs bought him. Everybody wanted him, and could have had him, but the other clubs remained on the sidelines. A wait-and-see attitude seemed the safest posture, despite Banks's talent.

Like the speculation surrounding Jackie Robinson's arrival in Brooklyn, rumors spread about whether fans would continue coming to the ballpark. Race riots would break out, especially if a black player got into a fight with a white player. Would the black fans rush onto the field or begin fighting white fans? It never happened, but there was a lot of talk about it.

By the late fifties the Negro Leagues had lost their talent. Most of the talent signed onto the Major League clubs. Negro League fans quit going to the ballpark. No more parades, no more rooting for the home Negro League team. The clubs finally folded in the early sixties.

Progress always has tradeoffs. Yes, it was right for integration to occur, but the price was the end of the Negro Leagues. Part of the fabric of solidity and pride disappeared in those communities after forty years.

9

Miles Behind, Miles Ahead, but No U-turns

For seventeen years Hughie knew only one employer, the Cleveland Indians. Work was steady. He got paid for doing something he loved. By 1952, thirty-four years old, divorced and with a daughter, he continued to rack up thousands of miles on the Great Plains, away from home for several days or even weeks at a time.

Moving through hundreds of ballparks confidently, he felt supremely delighted when other scouts, even veteran ones, looked up, wondering why he was in town. He craved attention and got it. He loved risk-taking and challenges. Other scouts respected him for what he had done and who he was.

Already known for his craftiness and outspoken behavior, Hughie nudged ahead. His life did not consist of U-turns, and he never uttered the lyrics of the old song "You Got It Made." Hughie would say that no one ever has it made. No one ever finishes paying his dues, whatever his fame. There will always be somebody watching, trying to dig into your mind. If you're successful, be prepared to be besieged by predators and copycats.

Hughie knew when he was being watched. Even when he pulled out a pencil and jotted a note on the flap of a popcorn box, eyes immediately turned to the field. The unspoken words were "Who's Hughie watching? Did he get a tip about somebody we don't know?"

During the fifties baseball took on a predictable course. One or two of the three New York teams usually appeared in the World Series. A lot of teams loaded up with home run hitters. Get a couple of guys on base, and then bring up your home run–hitting star. Stealing a base seemed foreign to the game, although there were some fast runners, like Mickey Mantle and Pedro Ramos. As Mantle years later remarked about Jose Canseco's 40/40 year (40 home runs and 40 stolen bases), if he had known it was so important, he would have stolen more bases.

Slowly baseball began changing, with increasing integration and the moving of franchises. What Hughie cherished as the permanence of tradition now collided with the forces of change. What would happen to the game, he didn't know. Attendance was dropping and not just because of the impact of television. By the end of the decade five franchises moved, beginning with the Boston Braves to Milwaukee in late 1952 and culminating with the Dodgers and Giants to the West Coast in 1958.

The ballparks in small towns showed no immediate change. The grandstands, rickety with bare wooden planks, remained intact. Small-town America, still vibrant, was home to 460 clubs in 1950, with 40 million paying customers. But by 1960 only twenty-two Minor Leagues remained. Many Minor Leagues, including the Negro Professional Baseball League, suffered slow deaths.

Baseball remained a daytime game. Doubleheaders, regularly scheduled, gave fans two for the price of one. Hughie still worked directly with kids and their parents with no intervening parties to muddy the waters—pure, unadulterated capitalism. Of course, the captains of baseball business held all the trump cards.

Although Cy Slapnicka returned to the Indians in 1947, many of his friends and contacts in the front office had left. It appeared that Slapnicka offered all the support Hughie needed to continue scouting with the Indians. But in 1952 Hughie resigned and headed for South Side Chicago. Hughie offered no answer for leaving the Indians. He may have gotten mad at somebody in Cleveland, wanted a raise, or just wanted a new challenge. No one but him knew with any certainty, and he wouldn't discuss the matter.

In 1950 Paul Richards, just four years removed from retiring as a catcher, had moved to Chicago to manage the White Sox. Richards and Hughie had known one another for a short time, and they lived but a couple of hundred miles apart. Both men, vigorous and highly opinionated, could be intimidating when anyone stood in their ways.

Richards and Frank Lane, the general manager of the White Sox, began talking to Hughie about coming to work with them. They knew his style of scouting. They felt that they could work with one another.

Certainly Hughie was impressed with Richards's baseball mind. As Jerome Holtzman wrote, "Richards's busy and fertile brain possessed more baseball knowledge than anyone since Branch Rickey." Like Rickey, Richards was a king of the art of persuasion. Veteran pitcher Saul Rogovin, recycled by the White Sox in the midfifties, remembered that "he conned all of us into thinking we were better than we were."

As tough-minded and self-assured as each was about himself, Richards and Hughie apparently had enough sense to set aside any negative thoughts and work together. An Oklahoman and a Texan were going to rebuild a team long dormant in the league.

Probably any question marks in Hughie's mind were about "Trader" Lane. Life was not going to be serene and predictable. He'd better strengthen his resolve without becoming exhausted around Lane.

With the White Sox Hughie kept his old scouting territory. Find the young talent, sign them, and who knows where they would be in a couple of years.

For the previous three decades the White Sox had wallowed near or at the bottom of the American League, twenty-four times since the infamous 1919 World Series. When Lane took over the reins of general manager in 1949 and hired Richards the following year, it was with the understanding that what Richards wanted, Lane tried to get.

What Richards wanted was speed, discipline, and some good pitchers. He handled the pitchers. No one in baseball was better at the job, at least in Richards's mind. Furthermore, no one disputed his word.

Within one year the White Sox competed for the pennant with speedy and defensive-minded players, notably with Nellie Fox, Eddie Robinson (one of the few offensive punches in the lineup), Chico Carrasquel, and Minnie Minoso. Now the Yankees' monopoly on the pennant was threatened by both Cleveland and Chicago.

Richards led the club, formerly known for finishes in the second division, to three consecutive years of third-place finishes. In 1954 the scrappy White Sox stayed in the race, while the Indians set a Major League record by winning 111 games in a 154-game season. In 1955 the White Sox fought the Indians and the Yankees down to the wire.

In his home territory Hughie began spending more time on college campuses. The University of Texas, Oklahoma A&M, the University of Oklahoma, and Texas Christian University continued to be hot spots for scouts. However, small towns stayed at the top of Hughie's list as a vast mother lode never to be overlooked.

Richards taught Hughie about what to look for in pitchers, invaluable advice that he used nearly ten years later to compete with Richards. They worked together for three years, until Richards accepted the job as manager and general manager of the new Baltimore Orioles in late 1955 and Hughie left the White Sox to join the Dodgers. Six years later Hughie and Richards met up again, this time as fierce competitors, when Richards built an expansion team, the Houston .45s, as general manager and manager.

White Sox general manager Frank "Trader" Lane was born with a roving eye. He seemed to be more interested in the players he didn't have than the ones he had. Hughie thought he woke up every morning saying, "Who can I trade today?" (Someone told Hughie years later that Lane made about five hundred trades as a team general manager.) He even dreamed up the idea of trading managers. Maybe he figured it was a lot easier making trades than looking for untested talent. Why give money to untested players who would spend three or four years in the Minors?

Lane (Mr. Wheeler-Dealer) would eventually leave the White Sox (after the '55 season, the same time Hughie did) to continue his front office theatrics in St. Louis. During his tenure there he traded Cardinal icon and future Hall of Famer Red Schoendienst to the New York Giants in a nine-player deal. However, the weirdest trade of all came in 1960, when he was general manager of the Indians. He swapped managers with the Tigers. The Indians got Jimmy Dykes; the Tigers got Joe Gordon.

Hughie's lessons about trading from Rickcy were reconfirmed by the Lane-Richards dynamic duo, particularly the lesson about one's attitude when entering the trading market. One goal was to see that their club and the club they were dealing with both became winners in trading. Then they could always come back a year later to talk about another trade. You just never knew who you might have to deal with in another month or another year. They all realized they should not close any doors and not be scared to trade a player. A lot of general managers are too scared to trade a player, because he might go to another club and show them up. That's fine, so long as the player he gets in return plays well also.

The three years with the White Sox, in retrospect, were formative ones for Hughie. The birth of the "Go-Go" White Sox was founded on trades to get Billy Pierce, Nellie Fox, and Minnie Minoso with pitching "retreads" Joe Dobson, Saul Rogovin, and Harry Dorish, prodding the South Side team to become a pennant contender. Pitching and hustling, two enduring trademarks of any Richards team, paid dividends when, fifteen years later, he used the same ideas with the Phillies.

During the '54 season Hughie got word that Richards was looking at a new opportunity—becoming general manager and field manager of the newly minted Baltimore Orioles. Lane and Charles Albert Comiskey II offered him a contract, but the chance to be boss on and off the field plus a salary hike appealed to Richards's ambitions. The Richardses of the baseball world don't stay in one place very long.

Perhaps Richards's leaving in late '54 and then hearing rumors that Lane would depart the next year propelled Hughie to look around. He got the message that wholesale changes in the Sox front office were coming. So he began checking around among his contacts at other clubs, one of whom was Lafayette Fresco Thompson, a vice president of the Brooklyn Dodgers who was in charge of their farm clubs.

As described by Harold Rosenthal, a beat reporter with the Yankees, Dodgers, Giants, and later the Mets, Thompson was "Southern-born, Northern-bred, and New York street-smarts, a proper mixture for survival." Fresco and Hughie probably met at scout meetings in the early fifties, when Fresco became a vice president after Walter O'Malley took over the Dodgers organization.

About ten years older than Hughie, Thompson came up to the Phillies as a player in the late twenties and quickly became a .300 hitter. Within two years he was team captain. Four years later the Phillies traded him and Frank "Lefty" O'Doul for four players and cash. Quipped Thompson, already known for his wit, "Every time pay day rolled around with the Phillies, they had to sell a player."

During the war Thompson hooked up with the Dodgers organization simply by asking Branch Rickey Jr. for a job in the farm system. Later, as farm boss, he analyzed regional reports about newcomers from scouts across the country. Undoubtedly Hughie's name popped up in conversations in Brooklyn between him and Al Campanis, also in the Dodgers' front office.

Hughie "knocked" on Fresco's door. He sold himself as the man to help Fresco build a new team, now composed of aging ballplayers. He got the job and kept his old scouting territory but did not get the moniker he desperately wanted—*Major League scout*.

10

First Brooklyn, Then Dodging His Way to the West Coast

"Boy, this is my happy day. I'm going to be home free." Hughie sang a song of happiness when he signed with the Brooklyn Dodgers in late 1955. The Dodgers then had about twenty-six farm clubs. That's about five hundred ballplayers.

He was going to have a picnic out here. "Damn, I'm going to sign players and see what they can do, because if they play well, they might have a chance." (Twelve of the Dodgers' farm clubs were Class D, the lowest; six, Class C. The remainder consisted of Single-A, Double-A, and Triple-A teams.)

What Hughie saw unfolding was a frightful Minor League trend. In 1949 fifty-nine Minor Leagues operated. By 1957 only twenty-nine remained. The constant decline alarmed Major League owners, and Thompson, Buzzie Bavasi, and Hughie were not indifferent to this dangerous trend.

Vanishing were teams and leagues in populous areas. The going-on-as-usual operations were not working, especially as the televising of Major League games hit attendance in these towns.

The question: How would the Major Leagues operate without the Minor Leagues? How would they develop young players? Where would the surplus talent go? And why would talented kids choose baseball if there was room for only a few?

A Major League club, according to Thompson, needed at least

twelve farm affiliates. Nevertheless, the short-term showed the Dodgers having lots of good players coming up. The number of standout rookies remained stable. What decreased were the run-of-the-mill prospects, as fewer were going into pro ball.

Hughie was determined to find the talent to feed the next generation of baseball fans. For nearly one hundred years of professional baseball, modest and great stadiums had been built and demolished. Fans, rich and poor, paid homage to the game with cash and passion. Now, with a booming postwar population and new franchises looking for Major League–caliber players with escalating bonus signings, Hughie's job took on greater demands as well as increased responsibility for spending the boss's money wisely with salaries going up.

In an ironic twist, the Dodgers also picked up Dale Mitchell from the Indians, whom Hughie signed seventeen years earlier. They would be together for only one year. In the '56 World Series Mitchell was the last batter to face Don Larsen when he pitched a perfect game. On a 3-2 count, Babe Parilli, the home plate umpire, called a high fastball "strike three." Striking out against Larsen was Mitchell's last appearance in a Major League uniform.

Hughie's first two years with the Dodgers (1956–57) were the last two for the club in Brooklyn. After several appearances in the World Series, Dodgers veterans Carl Furillo, Junior Gilliam, Carl Erskine, and Duke Snider were aging and on their way out. Rebuilding the club took on a greater urgency.

Walter O'Malley wanted out of Brooklyn after the site for a new ballpark was rejected. Attendance was down despite a pennant-winning 1956 season. Worn-out Ebbets Field lacked parking and space for expansion. O'Malley saw gold in southern California. To move to California, O'Malley had to have another club go with him. The baseball people told him that he couldn't move by himself. If you want to move to Los Angeles, we'll have to find another club to go with you.

O'Malley knew that Giants owner Horace Stoneham was broke.

He owed about ten years' back rent on the Polo Grounds. According to Hughie, O'Malley made a deal with Stoneham: to "loan" him $500,000 if he would move and also provide him with some expense money, because he damn sure couldn't move without it. Stoneham said okay and took the offer. He never repaid O'Malley. It was just a gift.

"Did the commissioner know about the loan? Yeah, but that didn't bother him because O'Malley really wasn't cheating. He was trying to help somebody out, and at the same time he was going to make millions and millions of dollars," remarked Hughie. The baseball owners wanted to go to the West Coast to expand Major League Baseball. Millions of new fans waited.

With Stoneham in San Francisco and O'Malley in Los Angeles, they had a lock on the Golden Bear state.

"What a helluva deal. Two big clubs with good records and, added attraction, the Dodgers-Giants feud would go on, but just six hundred miles apart," Hughie smiled.

O'Malley owned his own airplane, a twin-engine jet. He even had his own pilot. Whenever a club like the Giants got stranded somewhere, they called O'Malley, who sent the plane to pick them up and get them to a ballpark on time. How about that! Of course, he sent them a bill for services rendered.

The Dodgers kept its Vero Beach, Florida, spring training compound, using their blue jet to transport players. That plane was one of a kind. With it parked at the Dallas airport, one of Hughie's jobs was to act like a cruise ship agent, making sure that all the players got to the right gate and on board. In two days the Dodgers moved five hundred players in that plane. Pick them up, fly them to Vero Beach, return to Dallas, and pick up another batch.

In their new California cities, both clubs drew big crowds. The Dodgers played on a football field, the Los Angeles Coliseum. It was the strangest ball field ever imagined, with a big net erected in left field. Right field was so far away that "Vince Scully's descriptions were the only way fans 'saw' the game." The crowds in Los Angeles broke single-game records. Two years later O'Malley bought Chavez Ravine, just north of downtown. Up the road the Giants were preparing to open Candlestick Park.

The first season, 1958, in Los Angeles was lackluster. The Dodgers finished in seventh place. Sandy Koufax was the only pitcher to have a .500 record, and only Duke Snider hit .300. In the '59 season Dodger fortunes reversed themselves, because they made some good trades. They went on to win the NL pennant and bested the "Go-Go" White Sox four games to two in the World Series.

In 1960 the Dodgers got a lot of new faces, with Charlie Neal, Wally Moon, Frank Howard, and a new starter, Stan Williams. Within two years they were pennant contenders again, almost going to the World Series in 1962, but then they lost a playoff game to the Giants.

They stormed back in 1963 to win the pennant and sweep the Yankees in the World Series. In 1964 later they beat the Twins with three shutouts, but in 1966 the Orioles, backed by Jim Palmer, Boog Powell, Frank Robinson, and Brooks Robinson, jumped on the Dodgers to capture the World Series championship.

The year 1961 was not a fun year. Fresco Thompson was sick. The whole organization went haywire. Buzzie Bavasi, the general manager, saw the handwriting on the wall. The farm club system was a failure. What the Dodgers had done during the past couple of years was to make some trades by giving up young players.

Buzzie called a meeting in Los Angeles. He invited O'Malley, his son Peter, Fresco Thompson, Al Campanis, Bert Wells, and Hughie. He opened the meeting by announcing that the Dodgers had a horseshit scouting staff and a horseshit farm system.

"That's exactly what he said, and dammit, you could have heard a pin drop," remarked Hughie.

After a pause, Buzzie continued, "We are down in signing players." Then he announced what he wanted: "I want one hundred players signed during the coming year. I want at least one hundred players—I would like to have a few more, but I want one hundred."

"Al Campanis, the scouting director, jumped up out of his chair. I will never forget this, if I live to be 150 years old. He jumped up out of that chair and said, 'Buzzie, Buzzie, Buzzie!'" Hughie said.

"Yeah, Al, what's on your mind?"

"Do you have any idea what the penalty, what the repercussions might be if you sign that many ballplayers?"

"I don't give a damn what the repercussions are. I want at least one hundred players signed, and I'm going to allot $800,000 in bonuses. Here's something else. I want you right now to get a hold of your scouts and tell them that the two best scouts we got are Alexander and Bert Wells.

"They know what it is to scout a ballplayer, and they are the best finders in baseball when it comes to signing a player. And every time that any of our scouts get in the least bit of trouble in signing a player, I either want Hughie or Bert, or both of them, to go to that club that's got a hold of them, and fly them wherever you want them.

"Let them negotiate the damn deal on that ballplayer because they can handle it." Buzzie stopped, and the room remained silent. Hughie knew that he had earned Buzzie's trust, but he also knew that each day he had to earn it all over again.

Hughie would use the illustration that wildcat oil drilling in Oklahoma bears good news about 5 percent of the time. Hughie realized that the orders from Buzzie had the same odds in finding Major League players. Playing the odds with Lady Luck as a partner, working on hunches (none revealed), and looking for comforting answers that did not exist, Hughie knew but one goal. It was understood that Los Angeles fans wanted winning teams, or they wouldn't come out to the park. (Bavasi's orders paid off: in the sixties the Dodgers drew about 24 million fans.)

In 1961 expansion teams entered both leagues, and the hunt for more talent began earnestly in Panama, Venezuela, Nicaragua, the Dominican Republic, and Puerto Rico. Minor Leagues decreased and the Negro Leagues, depleted of their talent, folded. The scouts were instructed to keep after the old sources of players—high schools,

American Legion, JUCOs, and the industrial leagues—but to start looking at universities. Those were the marching orders.

With Buzzie's mandate, about 108 players signed. Still with a plentiful farm system, the Dodgers took some marginal players and made good trades. Trade three for one, or something like that. The Dodgers rebuilt their team quickly.

In 1962 the Dodgers were set to operate ten teams in their farm system, but then the Southern Association suspended operations. Now they had to find a place for those players. Quickly they decided to shift their franchise from Atlanta to Evansville, Indiana. Further creating havoc was the disbandment of the Three-I league for economic reasons. Not since the late 1930s had the Dodgers not had at least one club in every Minor League classification.

Although the Dodgers thought of colleges as an undependable source for new players, they had no alternative but to scout them, or somebody else would get the talent.

11

A Mythical Combination

His left name was Carl; his right name was Warwick. He confounded every scout except Hughie, because he threw left-handed and batted right. Guys with that kind of mythical combination are just too unusual. Hughie heard later that only a few men played in the Majors with those attributes—like Hal Chase and, later, Rickey Henderson.

When Hughie was with the White Sox he heard about this kid from Sunset High School in Dallas who hit two home runs and got seven RBIs in a championship American Legion summer league at Lagrave Field, home of the Fort Worth Cats of the Texas League. He put Warwick's name in his notebook to check up on him in a few months, as he already was recruited by TCU (Texas Christian University). An outfielder with good speed, Warwick racked up national honors his sophomore year, when TCU won the Southwest Conference title for the first time in twenty years and he was selected to the second team of the All-American team in 1956. The following year he made the first All-American team.

Other scouts headed for the TCU ball field to look at his unorthodox combination. They told him to try switch hitting, but he didn't have time. He could hit with some power, had good speed, and hustled, but all they wanted to know was how or why Warwick ended up a rightie at batting and a lefty at throwing. All he told them was, "I don't know. It just happened." The word among the scouts: we might take a chance to sign him, but not with any bonus money. He's too risky.

During the summer between Warwick's junior and senior year in 1957, Hughie heard that Carl was playing semipro with another prospect he was following, Gaylord Perry. He wanted to meet with Carl immediately.

However, Bavasi issued an edict about bonuses. What player positions do we need? Hughie had Warwick, Frank Howard, and a kid named Nicholson.

"They're all outfielders. Not interested. I might go with one or two," barked Bavasi.

Hughie went with Warwick and Howard.

Hughie called Warwick and asked to meet with him and his bride. They talked about what he wanted to do in baseball. Hughie asked his wife if she was willing to accept being a ballplayer's wife. She agreed. Nothing was mentioned about money.

A week later Hughie called, asking to meet at Warwick's parents' home in Dallas. Hughie arrived an hour early to get acquainted with Carl's mom and dad and ask them about their feelings if Carl left school to play baseball. They both were elated that Hughie wanted to sign him and give him a bonus, but again, no amount of money was mentioned until Carl and his wife arrived.

They sat down together in the living room as Hughie explained his offer. "Carl can get a $20,000 bonus and $5,000 a year for three years, and if he makes it to the Majors, there would be another $5,000." (As Carl said fifty years later, his folks fell in love with Hughie at that moment.)

"Now, what will Carl be making in the Minor Leagues?" Carl's father asked.

"Oh, about $500 a month," Hughie answered.

The father thought about it for several seconds. "That's not much to live on. How about $700 a month?" (What Carl learned later was that the $700 a month was just for six and a half months, not twelve, so he and his wife needed the $5,000 bonus money to live on.)

"Yes, that'll work. It's a done deal. I'll have the contract and check prepared," Hughie replied. He turned around to speak to Carl. "We both have something in your future and mine. What you do in baseball with the Dodgers depends if I'm still with them."

Hughie had a feeling that hell would break out in Los Angeles when the newspaper boys and other scouts heard about his signing a righty batter and a lefty thrower.

The next day he called Carl. "You created a storm. No one can believe that a ballplayer can get a $40,000 bonus. The newspapers are saying that Alexander is out of his mind."

When Hughie returned to Los Angeles, he knew that some of the Dodger scouts were talking to the press and feeding the writers all kinds of stuff, so he called them together and told them to knock it off. "The press can't hurt me, but they can do a lot of damage to this boy. Knock off the press leaks."

Just before Carl packed his bags to head for the Dodgers' Macon, Georgia, Class A club in the South Atlantic League, he called Hughie. "My wife and I were talking about needing another car to make the trip, so how about another $1,500 for a trade-in?"

There was a pause.

"Okay, it's a deal," Hughie replied.

Carl hit .279 and hammered 22 home runs in his first year. Danny Ozark, the Macon manager, took him under his wing and taught him to become a pull hitter, not just a straightaway hitter. His home run totals rang up sharply. The next year he hit 35 homers with Victoria in the Texas League and led the league with a .331 batting average.

The Dodgers, impressed with his hitting and fielding, called him up. In 1961 he headed for Los Angeles. On opening night he drove in two runs with a pinch-hit single. Later Buzzie Bavasi delivered the $5,000 bonus check. "Carl, maybe there is something about a right-handed hitter and a left-handed thrower. At least you got all the scouts' attention." Hughie beamed.

Carl's stay in Los Angeles was short-lived, as he was traded to the Cardinals, who then traded him to the Astros. By 1964 he returned to the Cardinals to play on their World Series championship team. In the first game he hit three for four, a pinch-hitting record, as the Cardinals beat the Yankees. For the next two years he flitted around with the Orioles and Cubs and a couple of Minor League clubs.

Years later Carl remarked that "Uncle Hughie" was the nicest guy he had ever met in baseball, like a second father. "Even before he signed me, he always walked over to my parents in the ballpark and talked awhile before sitting down to talk with me."

After Carl retired from baseball, he asked Hughie what he had written in his scouting report. Candidly, Hughie told him, "Accurate arm, great speed, power, and hustled constantly, always charging the ball, and doesn't make mistakes, at least no more than two times. If he didn't have the enthusiasm and hustle, he would just be an average ballplayer."

12

A Three-Traffic-Light Town
and Loads of Talent

Anadarko, Oklahoma, lies about sixty to seventy miles southwest
of Oklahoma City, a three-traffic-light town nestled in the rolling,
red clay hills. In the late 1950s and early '60s it was a hotbed of high
school and American Legion talent. The cream of the crop: Derrell
Griffith, Mack Kuykendall, and Johnny Bench.

In 1960 a high school coach called Hughie about a kid on his team
who could pound the ball. "He's a natural. You'll like him."

His name—Derrell Griffith. A couple of days later, Hughie arrived
in Anadarko to watch him play. "You talk about a hitter, he was a
natural .350 hitter. The whole town was full of scouts."

Hughie didn't talk much with Derrell but rather spent most of the
time with his dad and mom. They both told him how much their son
liked to play ball. They invited Hughie to dinner, and he arrived at the
Griffith home about 5:00 p.m. to talk about Derrell. Derrell's mom
just went out in the backyard to get a couple of chickens and soon a
heap of fried chicken, mashed potatoes, and gravy graced the table.

Several months later, after Derrell graduated from high school,
Hughie traveled to Anadarko and Chickapee to watch some American
Legion games. What a team! They pounded the ball everywhere.

The scouts poured into town again. Everybody heard about the
team and Derrell's hitting. They all thought they could get Derrell,
but when it came time for him to sign, nobody else had a chance.

"Nobody! I sat down with his dad and offered his son an $18,000 bonus, up front, right on the kitchen table," Hughie boasted.

Within a couple of months Derrell was off to Vero Beach, a kid taking his first airplane ride at age eighteen.

His first years were at Great Falls, Montana. He batted .313 and hit 14 home runs. The next year the Dodgers moved him up to Albuquerque, where he hit .286 with 20 homers. What a hitting show! The Dodgers called him up.

"He was a good infielder and could run like a rabbit. But he couldn't throw real well. He was just wild. Damn, he was wild. In one game he made six errors, all throwing errors. Finally the Dodgers sent different coaches to teach him how to throw," observed Hughie.

Hughie told the Dodgers that all that coaching was going to hurt his arm. "Leave him alone, or you're going to ruin him. Just leave him alone. If you keep working with him, you'll have him conscious of throwing the ball away every time he gets it. The he'll get to worrying that whenever a ball is pitched, it will be hit to him."

Although Derrell hit .290 for the Dodgers in '64, he bumped up and down from the Spokane and Albuquerque clubs until the end of the '66 season, when he was traded to the Mets along with Tommy Davis. Before the '67 season began, the Mets traded him to the Astros.

His last season was playing for the Austin club of the Texas League and the Oklahoma City 89ers of the Pacific Coast League. By that time he was married with a family and didn't want to travel anymore. So he quit baseball and returned home. The Dodgers later called him back, but he declined.

He returned to Anadarko, where he makes his home today.

Hughie's friends crossed several lines of the baseball world. Whenever he arrived in Oklahoma City to see the 89ers play, he would take two or three other scouts with him to eat his mother's cooking. After dinner they sat around telling baseball stories. Nieces, nephews, and even adult cousins sat attentively listening to Uncle Hughie's stories.

Excitement hit a new peak when famous ballplayers joined him, like Yogi Berra and Billy Martin. Famous players just sat around spinning stories in a modest house in Oklahoma City.

Whenever the children joined him at the ballpark, they knew their marching orders: "Do not talk to Uncle Hugh during a ball game. He is working." But before and after the game you could ask him questions. Sometimes they got crowded out because other scouts and front office people flocked around talking, shaking his hand, and wondering who he was scouting.

If the children asked how he evaluated a player, he demonstrated how a batter was to hold the bat, position his feet, and turn his body. Then he turned his attention to pitchers and how to grip a baseball and keep control. He didn't care for radar guns and stopwatches. What good is a radar gun if a pitcher has little control?

Then he spun stories about a lot of players he watched who had the talent but not the character to persevere when they hit a slump. How do you get to know a kid's character? Hughie learned that you spend time knowing his parents and friends. And they got to know Hughie. So if another club offered as much or even more money to a prospect, Hughie believed that he could still sign him, because he had taken the time.

13

Hondo Hits Them
High and Deep

Winner, South Dakota, is a dot on the south-central Dakota prairie just a few miles north of the Nebraska border. In the late fifties the population was about eight thousand, most of them rabid baseball fans.

One night during a game there in 1958, Hughie asked a couple where they were from. They named some town way off, and he asked where it was.

"It's about an hour-and-forty-five-minute drive from Winner."

Hughie told them that he had seen them at the ballpark the past couple of nights, and they quickly replied that they had season tickets.

"So you stay overnight?"

"Nope," they answered. "We come over here and drive back to the ranch, then get up in the morning, feed the cattle, do some chores, and then head back to Winner for another ball game."

Those people loved baseball.

The town had a little bar. In the back room gambling held sway—all kinds of gambling. Poker, dice—you name it, they had it, even slot machines. Hughie asked how they got by with all that stuff in there.

"Very easily," the reply came. "The sheriff loves baseball, and nobody can gamble except in that little back room. All the money that is made in the room goes to the ball club. That is a good place for it to go."

Bert Wells, a scout for the Dodgers, and Hughie traveled together a lot after the Dodgers' move to Los Angeles. Burt stood about five feet five and wore natty attire like pinstripe suits and spats. His signature statement was a pearl cigarette holder clinched in his teeth, much like Franklin Delano Roosevelt. His black hair glistened in the sunlight, and with a black pencil mustache, he stood like a miniature Clark Gable.

If baseball had an odd couple, Hughie and Burt topped the charts. In middle America they cast a Mutt and Jeff caricature, with every eye on them as soon as they walked into a ballpark or beer joint.

Bert was a good man. He and Hughie were what Latinos call simpatico, having a sense that even unspoken thoughts are understood. He used to tell Buzzie and Campanis when Hughie wasn't around about how good Hughie was in signing players. "He's the best scout in baseball, and he can sign a ballplayer better than anybody else in baseball."

"Really? You're bragging on me?" Hughie innocently replied.

Later Campanis and Buzzie made a deal that Bert and Hughie could work together. Bert would call Hughie up and say, "Hey, you, I've got a ballplayer; I'm going to struggle with him and might lose him. Can you take a little time and come help me try to sign him? Because you're damn good . . . you really know how to sign a player."

"You're damn right, I will. I'll come help you."

Bert and Hughie journeyed to Winner to see an outfielder, a big guy playing on the Rapid City team. His moniker was Hondo, his birth name, Frank Howard. The club played some of their games in Winner and other small towns. Hughie's job was to scout Howard, while Burt headed to another town to look at another player.

That night Howard hit four home runs in a doubleheader, all over the light towers in left and left-center field. He hit the ball out of sight and into the darkness. Boy, he was a strong kid, six feet six and probably weighed 260 pounds. He was treacherous with the bat.

After trying to get hold of Bert, Hughie finally called the Rapid City club manager to be sure that Bert saw Howard. "Take good care of Howard, as we are going to try to sign him," Hughie repeatedly told the manager. "And get in touch with Bert."

Hughie injected a sense of urgency into signing Hondo. Like a Christmas shopper at 3:00 a.m. on Black Friday, he always figured he had only a few hours to close a deal before other scouts scrambled into town.

Hughie had learned that timing is everything. He claimed he learned that lesson from the carnival days. Whether a hot prospect or a customer in line to see fleas dance, everybody likes to think he's getting a deal. Only the paying customer counts.

The Dodgers ended up giving Howard a $108,000 bonus. Another club offered him $120,000, but Bert and Hughie had the inside track. He liked them and the Dodgers.

"We were surprised when he just came up to our room and said he wanted to sign," remarked Hughie.

"I want to sign with you guys. If you give me a good enough deal, I'll sign and it doesn't have to be as much as some other clubs have offered me," Howard said.

"How much do you want?" Hughie asked.

"$108,000," he replied.

"We're going to give that to him, aren't we, Bert?" Hughie asked.

"Oh, yeah," Bert answered.

"Now, I'm going to take the $100,000, and I'm going to give my mother and dad $8,000 for a down payment on a house, a little home for them," Howard explained.

"By God, that's good, I like that!" Hughie exclaimed.

Howard signed that night.

The other scouts got ticked off at Bert and Hughie, but the duo did their homework. They had the right connections, and Hondo liked the Dodgers.

The Dodgers asked Guy Welmand, a teacher and part-time scout for them in the Chicago area (he had played some ball in the Dodger organization), to manage the Rapid City club and take care of Howard. Guy took the offer quickly.

"I always stand behind my boys. I'd be talking to the mother. Damn, I could really handle mothers, and I bet 75–80 percent of the time,

1. Hugh Alexander: A stick of dynamite. Courtesy
Dan Austin.

2. (*Left*) Cy Slapnicka: Twice he changed Hughie's life.

3. (*Above*) Allie Reynolds: The first player Hughie signed, thanks to Hank Iba.

4. Dale Mitchell: Fleet of foot and a good batting eye,
based on a bartender's tip.

5. Gene Bearden: Hughie traveled to Arkansas to find a first baseman; instead he found a pitcher who led Cleveland to a pennant and World Series championship.

6. Paul Richards: He taught Hughie how to scout
pitchers and later became his nemesis.

7. Carl Warwick: Hughie thought an odd baseball superstition held no merit.

8. (*Left*) Derrell Griffith: Anadarko, Oklahoma, became a gold mine in Hughie's backyard.

9. (*Above*) Frank Howard: Hondo hit them high and far in the wheat fields of South Dakota.

10. Dick Calmus: His mother wanted not one but both sons to play ball, so Hughie signed them.

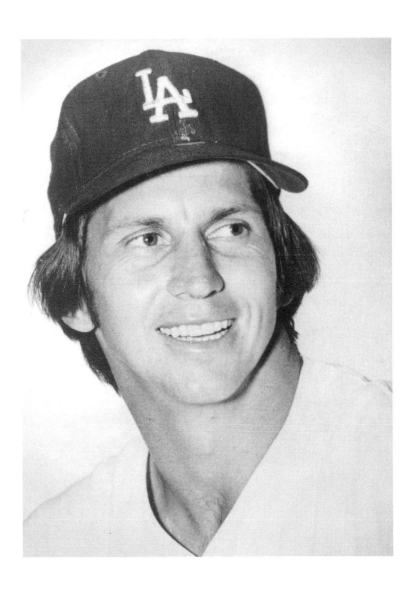

11. Don Sutton: The Dodgers said no initially, but
Hughie interceded for a future Hall of Famer.

12. (*Above*) Tommy Dean: The Astros were determined to sign him, so Hughie dreamed up a tax scheme.

13. (*Right*) Paul Owens: Friendship begets trust to make the Phillies a championship team.

14. (*Above*) Dallas Green: A master of building a farm system who learned the art of scouting from Hughie.

15. (*Right*) Marty Bystrom: Many clubs wanted him, but only Hughie knew the one question to ask about the amateur draft system.

TEAM _Phil. Phillies_   COACH   DATE 4/16-17-18 13-15 22/9/0

NO.	NAME	POS	AGE	HT	WT	CL	B	T	A	F	R̄	4	P	
4	Lenny Dykstra	8	✓				L	L				✓		Great
12	Mickey Morandini	4	✓				L	R				4		Good
7	Mariano Duncan	476	✓				R	R				No		Good
15	Dave Hollins	3	✓				S	R				4		Good
10	Darren Daulton	RH	✓				L	R				4		Good
8	Jim Eisenreich	9	✓				L	L				4		Good
13	Chas Hayes	5	✓				R	R				No		OK
27	Lenny Webster	2	✓				R	R				No	f.b.- back up
19	Kevin Stocker	6	✓				S	R				4		Good
2	Rick Holifield	8	✓				L	L				4		prospect
12	Doug Weathington	5	✓				R	R				No	Ext man
6	Tony Longmire	79	✓				L	R				No	Put man
55	Gene Schall	3	✓				R	R				4		prospect
31	Randy Ready	4	✓				R	R				No	E-H man
21	Tom Marsh	9	/				R	R				No	AAA

Form 313

16. (*Left*) Ron Clark: One of Hughie's legacies, a ballplayer who learned the fine art of scouting.

17. (*Above*) Educated guessing about a ballplayer's chances for success: Hugh Alexander's quest for certainty.

NO.	NAME	POS	AGE	HT	WT	CL	B	T	A	F	R	4	P	
25	Devon White	8	✓				S	R					4	Great
12	Roberto Alomar	4	✓				S	R					4	Great
19	Paul Molitor	DH	✓				R	R					4	Good
29	Joe Carter	7	✓				R	R					4	Great
9	John Olerud	3	✓				L	L					4	Great
33	Ed Sprague	5	✓				R	R					4	OK
15	Shawn Green	9	✓				L	L					4	Great prospect
8	Alex Gonzalez	6	✓				R	R					4	Good
27	Randy Knorr	2	✓				R	R					4	OK
53	Angel Martinez	2	✓				L	R					No	great arm
17	Robt Perez	7 pH	✓				R	R					NO	AAA
29	Lonell Roberts	8-7	✓				L	R					No	Speed
51	Tilson Brito	4	✓				R	R					4	good prospect
6	Carlson Delgado	3 DH	✓				L	R					4	Can hit with power - poor catch
14	Howard Battle	5	✓				R	R					4	good prospect

TEAM Tor Blue Jays   COACH   DATE 4/13 - 14

Form 313

18. (*Above*) Sometimes Hugh was right; other times the crystal ball was murky.

19. (*Right*) Hugh Alexander in the late 1980s, at his fiftieth anniversary as a scout. Courtesy Dan Austin.

when you're going to sign a young player, the mother always makes the final decision. Did you know that? The mother always ends up making the final decision—most of the time." Hughie constantly sang that song, maybe a different verse, about mothers.

"I've racked my brain so many times. I'd be driving down the highway and I'd say, 'Dammit, I'm not too sure that the mother is going to handle this deal.' It might be a deal I'm a little skeptical of. And I say, 'I'm going to go along with it. I haven't failed yet.'

"I knew way back there that so many scouts work their damn britches off. You know, to be sure, they would see a mother in the ballpark, you know, and all that bullshit. They just couldn't bullshit as I could. That's what it amounted to.

"Talk to mama. Talk to mama. If her boy was going to Kokomo, Indiana, she didn't know what kind of city it was, so I had to convince her that the Dodgers and I would take care of that boy. I don't care whether they played that good or not. I'd call the mother on the phone about once a week and find out about her boy. I wanted everything to be all right."

Hughie repeated the story about mamas to anyone who would listen. "And I always asked, 'Can I help you in any way?' That's my number-one winning strategy."

In 1960 Hondo was named NL rookie of the year and became a mainstay of the rebuilding efforts by the Dodgers' front office. Hondo tore up the ballparks, a big dude launching tape-measure home runs. Always in the top ten in slugging percentage, on-base percentage, runs scored, and RBIs, he stood in the ranks of power hitters with Hank Aaron, Harmon Killebrew, Willie Mays, Willie Stargell, Richie Allen, and Frank Robinson during the sixties and early seventies.

But at the end of the '64 season he was traded to the Senators. In May 1968 he tore up American League pitching by belting ten home runs in twenty at bats, hitting at least one home run in six consecutive games.

In 1973, after getting no bids from Major League clubs, he played a short stint in Japan and returned home.

14

Getting a Twofer

"You better hurry, or Paul Richards [then general manager and field manager of the expansion club the Houston Colt .45s] is gonna sign this Dick Calmus, out of Tulsa. He's a good little pitcher." The caller's voice sparked with urgency.

Hughie hustled over to Tulsa High School to get acquainted with Calmus and his parents. He had a helluva job on his hands, because Paul Richards had an edge on him from recruiting the boy's high school coach and had promised the coach a new Pontiac if he'd help him sign Dick.

Richards had a knack of complicating Hughie's life, because no one was shrewder in judging pitching talent. Richards moved from the White Sox to take a hapless St. Louis Browns team to Baltimore. Focusing on pitching, he built a team that had always been in last place into one of respectability, led by Hoyt Wilhelm. When the Orioles improved, Judge Roy Hofheinz recruited Richards as general manager of the Colt .45s, much closer to his Texas home.

Now, in 1961, Richards and Hughie matched wits in signing raw talent. Wherever Richards lingered, Hughie had his hands full.

Finally Hughie got a chance to sit down with Dick's parents at the ballpark, and a few days later he asked them if he could be the last scout to meet with them to discuss their son's baseball future.

Several days later Hughie walked inside the Calmus home after being greeted by a distraught Mrs. Calmus. Tears ran down her face. She got her apron wet just wiping her tears away.

"What's the matter, Hon?" Hughie put his arms around her.

She replied that the Houston club offered Dick $100,000 but they didn't want to sign her older boy, Merle. (Merle loved baseball and wanted to be a pitcher, but he couldn't pitch.)

"What!" Hughie said. She told him to sit down. He thought quickly that if he didn't sign both boys, he wasn't going to sign either one of them.

"Would you sign Merle?" she asked.

"I'll sign both boys for $60,000. If I don't get both boys, I ain't going to sign either one of them. I'm just going to walk out." He was bluffing and hoped that it would pay off.

"Well," she replied, "you gonna sign them, 'cause we're going to do it right now."

She was right.

When Paul Richards caught up with him later, Hughie told him that he had just signed them.

"Ah, bullshit! I don't believe a word you're telling me," remarked Richards.

"Paul, I just signed them!" Hughie boasted.

Boy, Paul was mad. He told Hughie the older boy couldn't pitch.

"I didn't give a damn whether he can or not. He's signed," Hughie exclaimed as he walked to his car.

Dick Calmus, a six-foot-four, right-handed pitcher, at age eighteen got shipped off to Keokuk, Iowa, in the Class D Midwest League. In his first year he got a respectable 8-4 record. In 1963, when he only was nineteen years old, the Dodgers brought him up and he earned a 3-1 record with a 2.66 ERA, while the Dodgers swept the Yankees in the World Series. After the '63 season the Dodgers sent him to the Albuquerque club, where he joined the army reserve. The Dodgers got upset and traded him to the Cubs in 1967. Two years later Calmus hung up his cleats.

15

He Made Me Keep
Coming Back

"Yes, Branch Rickey told me if I couldn't make up my mind about a player, 'Walk away, walk away,'" Hughie mused. "But there was a kid down in San Antonio I was scouting that had me coming back again and again, at least six times, before I could make up my mind. There was something that kept gnawing at me about the kid."

Billy had a remarkable trait that a lot of natural athletes never learn: that to hit consistently, a player has to forget his failures earlier in the game or yesterday. If failure creeps into his head, he loses control, and a vicious, unrelenting cycle begins that causes a loss of focus when he steps into the batter's box. Somewhere Billy learned to discipline his mind to overcome the fear of failure.

A "bird dog" told Hughie about Billy Grabarkewitz, an All-American out of St. Mary's University in Texas. He knew that the Braves and the Tigers were interested in the kid because he could play any infield position. No question that Billy would go high in the draft.

After visiting with his parents, Hughie learned that Billy wanted to go with the Dodgers, not any other team. Everybody in town knew that Billy wanted to be a Dodger and he wouldn't sign with any other club. So Hughie offered him $9,000 after the Dodgers drafted him in the amateur draft in 1966. He signed.

Did he get him on the cheap? Hughie would not say, although later

he heard he had gained a new moniker: "The One-Armed Bandit."
Hughie shrugged his shoulders at the questionable label.

From 1966 thru 1969 Billy played in the Minors, beginning with
the Class A Tri-City Atoms (Richland, Kennewick, and Pasco, Wash-
ington) in the Northwest League, then climbing to Spokane in the
Pacific Coast League. He batted about .270, except with Albuquerque,
when he hit .308 in 1968.

Finally, in 1970 Billy landed on the Dodgers' roster, although he
had broken his ankle the year before. That was his best year in the
Majors, when he batted .289.

"A damn good infielder," Hughie remembered. "He could play
position, and even in the outfield. That's the kind of boy a manager
needs. Put him in the game and he'll play sharp defense," Hughie
mused, justifiably proud.

In 1973 Billy and Hughie hooked up again for a year when he was
traded to the Phillies by the Angels. At the end of the '74 season the
Phillies traded him to the A's, where he played but six games before
being sent to the Tucson club.

If he hadn't had the injuries, he could have played several more
years as his defense improved.

At first glance Iuka, Mississippi, is just another sleepy little southern
town. It lies on the border with Alabama in the northeastern part
of the state. Like hundreds of other small towns that populate the
landscape of the Deep South and Midwest, Iuka has no traffic lights,
just a flashing yellow light at a school crossing. Freight trains roar
by on the outskirts of town.

In the early sixties, with a population of about three thousand,
Iuka didn't even have a proper ball field. Kids who wanted to play
organized ball had their parents take them down the road to Boon-
eville, thirty miles away.

Hughie got a tip about a Tommy Dean, as good a fielding shortstop
as you ever wanted to see. Everybody was after him. Tommy, a big

kid, played basketball on the high school team. During his junior year one of his teammates died on the court, so the school administration made all the athletes take physical exams.

Tommy failed his because of high blood pressure, and no one could figure out why. His parents sent him to Natchez for some medical tests and the doctors found that he had only one kidney. He was born with one kidney.

Later his older brother confided in Hughie about Tommy's condition. "Do you think that'll bother his baseball career?" his brother asked.

"I didn't know. I'll call an urologist in Oklahoma City, a friend of mine."

"It'd hurt him if he got a real bad hit. There are a lot of people who go through life with just one kidney and don't even know it. He can play ball and do anything else," the urologist reported.

A lot of scouts were after him. To get his attention, Hughie decided to help the whole family in some imaginative ways, especially after talking with his brother, who was giving Tommy lots of advice. Why, Hughie even tutored Tommy's little sister with her homework.

A couple of months later Hughie called Al Campanis back in Los Angeles to discuss signing the boy. "I better go with you and help you try to sign him," Al remarked.

"I wanted to say that I didn't want any of his damn help, but he was my boss," Hughie recounted later.

A couple of days later Hughie picked up Al in Memphis and drove him to Iuka. They checked into a motel and drove over to Tommy's home to talk with his father.

"You're going to be the last scout to meet with Tommy, and then we'll make a decision, so why don't you come out to the house about 5:00 p.m. tomorrow?" said his father.

"Okay," Hughie replied.

The next day Al and Hughie started out to the house. "You really screwed up this deal," Al complained. "By the time we get there, the boy will already be signed. All the other scouts, including Paul

Richards, will have already met with him and any one of them will sign him and I made a trip halfway across the country for nothing."

"Al, you were born in Greece and raised in New York City. You don't know how farm people operate. Their word is good, and don't you believe that it isn't. I'll bet you anything you want that when we get there, he will not be signed until we get through with him. I'll buy you a fifth of whiskey if I'm wrong." Hughie knew he was right.

Al and Hughie pulled up in front of the Dean home. Who was there, grinning and confident? Paul Richards, just waiting for Hughie to show him up.

"Go on in there go and get it over with because I'm going to sign that ballplayer in a few minutes. Houston has given him a hell of an offer." Richards believed the negotiating was over and he had won.

What Richards and Campanis didn't know was that several days earlier Hughie had gone to Memphis and stopped by the regional office of the IRS to talk with one of their guys. He didn't tell the IRS boys all the details but asked, "If I sign a ballplayer and his brother taught him how to play baseball and worked with him all those years, do you think the IRS would go along with me giving the boy X amount of dollars and giving his brother half the money? In other words, if I wanted to sign him for $60,000, do you think the IRS would approve $30,000 for him and $30,000 for his brother, because they live in the same house?"

This IRS man said that they didn't have rule about that kind of situation. Hughie walked out of that IRS office and kept saying to himself, "They don't have a rule, they don't have a rule, or he would have told me. They don't have a rule. They might make one when I get through, but they don't have a rule. And I'm going to use it right to the hilt."

Tommy opened the screen door and invited them in.

"Well, Mr. Richards offered me a $100,000 bonus," Tommy announced.

"You can't, Tommy. Here's the way it is. Tommy, you and your mother and dad and sisters and your brother—you're not going to make Mr. Campanis and the Dodgers pay $40,000 more. You like the Dodger organization and we like you."

Tommy replied, "I don't want to, but $40,000 is a lot."

Hughie responded, "I'm going to show you the breakdown on income. If you take $100,000, and you have to take it in a lump sum, I'm going to show you how much tax you're going to pay, but I'm also going to show you how much you and your brother would have to pay if I split the money between the two of you. And the difference is going to be $5,600. You're not going to make me and the Dodgers pay that extra $40,000 so you can recover $5,600. It's only fair because your brother taught you to play baseball."

Tommy nodded. "Right! Dad, I want to sign with Mr. Alexander."

When Hughie went outdoors, Paul Richards beamed, then blew up when Hughie told him he just signed Tommy. He said, "Oh, bullshit!"

"Well, go inside and ask him."

"How much did you give him?" asked Richards.

"I'm not going to tell you.

A couple of minutes later, Richards stormed out the door. "Well, I'll be a son of a bitch. How did you sign that ballplayer for $60,000, and I offered him $100,000?"

"Did you ever hear about income tax?" Hughie smugly offered. (Although not knowledgeable about tax laws, Hughie figured that splitting the bonus money between two guys put them in a lower tax bracket.)

Tommy broke in with the Dodgers in 1967 and then was traded to the Padres in 1969. Although he was a weak hitter, he compensated by being a respectable infielder in his four-year Major League career.

16

From No Prospect to Future Hall of Famer

The year: 1972. Don Sutton, resolute and unfaltering, pitched his best season. Posting a 2.08 ERA and 9 shutouts, he started 30 games and hurled 270 innings. For sixteen years he hurled for the Dodgers (1966–80), never spending one day on the disabled list. He knew how to keep in peak condition, mentally and physically.

In 1998 he got the phone call. "Congratulations, you have been elected into the Baseball Hall of Fame."

Don Sutton's entry into professional baseball was no easy task. No scout took him seriously, but one returned to take a second look, Hughie Alexander. Years later, as a broadcaster, Sutton acknowledged Hughie's belief in him.

Building a farm system involved more than just signing players. Sometimes it was finding new towns where baseball had deep roots. On the Dodgers' priority list was Rapid City, South Dakota. They liked the town because the people there loved baseball. It was in 1964 that Bert Wells and Hughie worked on the deal, paying $4,000 to set up a farm club there and then paying Marty Bascomb a salary to manage the club.

"Hughie, you need to look at this young fellow right away, a pitcher. His name is Don Sutton." Marty had a hot tip and wanted Hughie to get to Rapid City ASAP. Neither Bert nor Hughie had ever heard of him.

Well, they saw him pitch and he didn't look too bad. He didn't look great, but not real bad. His fastball was average but he had a way above average curve. Hughie told Sutton that they would get back to him, while also trying to get him on one of the semipro teams playing in the Wichita tournament in late August. He could pick up a couple of hundred dollars.

Hughie called a friend who managed the Midland, Michigan, semipro team. They always did one another favors, and the manager got all excited about having Sutton on the team. He would call Sutton. So Hughie offered the manager about $300, of which $200 was to go to Sutton. Bring him to Wichita, the site of the best semipro tournament in the country.

Sutton pitched a helluva game in Wichita. He was faster than Hughie remembered, and his curve ball was at peak form. He struck out eighteen players that night. About fifteen to twenty scouts watched him, but nobody knew anything about Don Sutton except Bert and Hughie, and they knew only a little bit. The next morning all these scouts, including Bert and Hughie, gave him an NP—no prospect.

Why a change of heart overnight? Because Al Campanis said no, and the reason was that Leon Hamilton, a Dodger scout in the Southeast, had already turned Sutton down.

"Oh, bullshit," Hughie hollered. "That's not the right way to handle this."

They argued a long time over signing Sutton, but Al wouldn't budge. "That got our dander up, and we fought for him."

Then they did something: they went over Al's head and talked to Buzzie. Bert and Hughie had a lot of pull, so to speak, with the Dodgers front office. They always knew they could go all the way to Buzzie if they had to. They weren't going to walk away. They fought back. You're damn right, they fought back.

"Buzzie, I hate to do this, because it has nothing to do with Al. It's the scout who turned him down. Al doesn't want to make Leon look bad. To hell with that!" Hughie tried to be diplomatic.

Then Hughie came up with a deal. "You let us get in the act and

Bert and I will relinquish our claim, so to speak, with Sutton, and we'll make the whole deal up, type the contract and the whole works, and send them to Leon Hamilton and let him do the actual signing. We'll just do the favor."

What the hell! Baseball people, they all knew what happened. Hughie knew that Buzzie would give them the approval.

That was the plan. Sutton wanted $20,000, which was pretty high for a ballplayer with a no prospect tag on him, but Hughie and Bert thought he was worth it.

A week or so after the tournament, Don went home. "We got a deal for you and we're going to send Leon Hamilton over and actually sign you up," Hughie told him.

"You better not send me Leon Hamilton because my dad will throw his ass right out the front door. Leon had made a statement that my dad didn't like when I was pitching a couple of years earlier," Sutton remarked.

Nevertheless, Leon headed over to the Sutton home. When Don's father opened the door and saw who it was, he slammed it shut.

Finally, Hughie and Bert asked Buzzie to send Marty Bascomb to the Sutton home. Marty was a different type of guy. The Dodgers needed him to sign Sutton. The plan worked.

Don Sutton was a real competitor. He was a kid that, when you talked to him, would say with certainty that he was going to pitch in the big leagues, regardless of what some of the scouts said.

Later, in the middle of his career, he used a spit ball. His fastball went down, and he had to throw curve after curve mixed with a change-up. So he started spitting on the ball, or however, he doctored it up. A lot of people didn't like that too well.

But he wanted to stay in baseball, make a lot of money, and make a big name for himself. He was that kind of kid . . . and still is.

17

Where There's a Tryout Camp, There's Hope

"Hey, guys, get in line. Get a number, and if you can't remember it, tape it to the bill of your cap, write it on your hand, on your glove. Your number is called twice. That's it." Hughie barked and cussed at everybody at a tryout camp.

"Okay, now get in line. We're going to time you in the 60-yard dash."

"All right, you five, get over by the batting cage."

"Pitchers, over here by the third base dugout! Catchers, behind home plate. Outfielders, down the left-field line. Infielders, over by first base."

Whistles blew incessantly as players ran around. How everyone got into his position, no one knows. Play begins. It's big. It's exciting. Every kid wants to jump from an anonymous number to a recognized name.

Tryout camp—it's like a cattle call for one hundred kids making their first or last debut. Everyone knows the risks but keeps hoping for that first break. It's the beginning of the journey to the Big Show or back to the sandlot. Anybody short of the handicapped could try out—the well-built, the short, the lean, and the pudgy wearing a motley collection of uniforms.

"Why do ballplayers come to a tryout camp? It must be the love of the game. It certainly can't be hoping to be picked up by a team, because the chances of surviving are slim to nil." Hughie let down his guard speaking to a small-town reporter.

Hughie's first encounter with tryout camps occurred in Springfield, Ohio, in 1938, the ballpark that he had played in the year before. Slapnicka wanted him to look at some player. As he sat at the front gate registering the players, a big dude stood in front of him.

"Name," Hughie ordered without looking up.

"Bob Lemon," the eighteen-year-old kid replied.

"Okay. What position?"

"Third base, center field, and pitcher," Lemon said.

"Okay, stand over there!"

Yes, it was future Hall of Famer Bob Lemon. Hughie signed him up, that is, for tryout camp.

Tryouts gained notoriety in the late forties when Branch Rickey made a deal with *Argosy*, a sports magazine, to have tryout camps every weekend across the country. From New York to Los Angeles a couple of Dodger scouts and a small group of *Argosy* employees set up camps. Everything was *Argosy*/Dodgers.

When a camp was over, they pulled up stakes and headed for another town. If the scouts liked somebody, one of them stayed behind to try to sign the player or at least take a couple extra looks at him. Then the scouts raced to the next town to begin the process all over again.

A few times Hughie watched the camps and was amazed at what the Dodgers and *Argosy* did. The Dodgers had twenty-nine farm clubs and needed players, and to show how sharp Rickey was, he probably told the magazine owners how they could get a lot of publicity. He probably told them he didn't have much money, so the full freight was on *Argosy*'s account. Rickey was pretty tight with money.

The kids who showed up bought the next issue of *Argosy* hoping to find their picture. It was a far-fetched idea. It was like throwing money out the window. Some players were offered contracts. Whether or not they were any good, Hughie did not remember.

Years later Hughie tried his hand at conducting some camps. If they weren't organized properly, they would just go to hell. The first thing he did was to advertise in the newspapers and on local radio stations. Most of the time he didn't have to buy time or space, because in smaller towns they just jumped at the chance to tell everyone that some Major League tryouts were coming to town.

In the early sixties he held camps in Kilgore, Texas, and the newspaper began calling them the Dodger Town Trial Camp. Anyway, it would draw from one hundred to three hundred ballplayers (or wannabe players).

Setting up a camp was tiresome and filled with grunt work. It was the same old routine. Hughie told the guys with him about what had to be done. Get them at the ballpark no later than 7:30 in the morning. Some of the players arrived early, so the orders were no one is allowed on the field. Make them sit in the stands, and at the right time they can come down on the field one at a time, where each one registered: name, address, telephone (if any), and birth date.

It took a lot of time to register each kid. Afterward they gathered the kids around home plate or in the grandstand to get a little talk about what was expected of them for the next two days.

"We'll play a ball game tomorrow, going about fifteen or twenty innings, and my rules go. Whatever my rules are, that's what goes. If I say we're going to have six outs in this inning, we're not going to go for three, we're going for six."

A lot of times the crew gave Hughie more trouble than the players. Andy Andrews, one of the crew, never paid any attention to the rules. It's a wonder anybody didn't get hurt. Doug Gassaway, he would do anything Hughie asked him. Finally Hughie had to tell the others to go home if they didn't like the way the camp was run.

One thing that surprised Hughie was that some players followed him from one camp to another. They showed up in Kilgore, then came over to eastern Louisiana, and a week later would show up at another camp. Maybe they just liked to be around baseball people.

A few were the older, gifted players who wanted to give it one more try. Their friends and relatives kept nagging them to go out just one more time. They'd had their day in the sun, but the hypnotic call beckoned them.

One Saturday morning when Doug, the rest of the crew, and Hughie were leaving the hotel, he got an important long-distance call. "You guys go on over to the field and get things ready. I'll get rid of whoever it is, but the call's important." Hughie seemed irritated by the interruption.

When Hughie finally got to the ballpark, it was bedlam. There must have been fifty balls being thrown and batted around. And one guy was walking down to first base, not doing a damn thing.

"What the hell's going on? We're going to get somebody killed throwing all those balls all over the outfield and infield. All you're doing is chewing tobacco."

Hughie's face turned a bright red as he chewed and cussed them out. When he finished he turned around to find a priest standing right behind him.

"Are you Hugh Alexander?" the priest asked.

"Yeah, that's me," Hughie replied.

"I've been hearing a lot of cussing language from you, and I'm preaching a sermon tomorrow morning at church. I think it would help you a lot to come up and listen."

Hughie was a little embarrassed. He just hadn't known a priest was near him. Embarrassed, Hughie stood speechless, a rare moment of silence.

A lot of the kids simply didn't know how to play. Why have them spend a lot of money and time to pursue a dream that was not to be? Sometimes he'd take a few minutes and ask each one if he had the ambition to become a ballplayer. The answer was always yes.

"Think about it. You ought to go to school or college or something."

Hughie struggled for the right words, anything to make the kid feel better. Yes, even a little bullshit. Always be a politician. It wasn't easy.

When Hughie held a tryout camp in Albuquerque, New Mexico, in the early sixties he got hit with a fine from the commissioner.

Otherwise, it was a good camp, not a great one. He and his crew were looking at a lot of Mexican ballplayers.

One of the first rules about organizing a tryout camp was to be sure there was plenty of food at lunch time. Coming into a town, Hughie's first job was to make a deal with a local restaurant, not a big fancy one. Fix up a couple-hundred ham sandwiches, some milk and soda, and some apples or oranges.

The restaurant owner had orders to deliver them before noon; otherwise, the deal was off. If you have a hundred boys playing ball all morning, they're going to be hungry. You can't have them running all over town, wasting a lot of time.

The commissioner had a strict rule that ballplayers couldn't work out unless each one had written permission from his coach or American Legion post commander. If he didn't have permission, up in the grandstand he went.

On day one boy in the stands arrived without a permission slip. At lunch time the staff served food to everyone, including that one boy. Hughie wasn't just going to leave him out. That's the way he played the game. No one was going hungry. Someone turned Hughie in to the commissioner, and he was fined $500. Fresco Thompson got mad and read the riot act to the commissioner's office. "Alexander is not going to pay that fine," an infuriated Thompson hollered. He didn't.

Hughie enjoyed the camps, until the draft system appeared in the mid-1960s. When the draft hit, that took care of the tryout camps.

When he joined the Phillies in 1971 he handled a few camps but limited them to one hundred players. Later he invited some college coaches to attend at the club's expense, because he knew they could help the club later.

"You can sit in the grandstand, but don't go down on the field to try to recruit anybody, or I'll kick your ass out of the park. After the camp is over, they can talk all you want.

By letting the coaches talk with the boys after the camp was over, Hughie won something, and that was good tips. If a college coach offered a scholarship to a boy, Hughie checked up on him one or two years later.

"Coach, this is Hughie. How about that boy you watched at the Kilgore tryout camp last year? How's he doing?"

"Hughie, the kid has a good arm but needs to work on hitting. Another year, if he's still interested in ball, I'll give you a call," the coach typically answered.

Hughie had a well-oiled network. The big schools—like Texas, Oklahoma, and LSU—he knew their coaches, and he gave them recommendations from the tryout camps. A lot of kids had a chance to become a ballplayer, but they weren't ready yet to go out and play professionally. Instead, he lined them up with the college coaches to go to school on a scholarship. Everybody became a winner.

18

Make Way for Tomorrow

"Make your own kind of music," the Mamas and the Papas sang. "Sing your own special song. Make your own kind of music even if nobody else sings along." Club owners felt the song's message as it reverberated through the counterculture movement of the sixties and seventies. Do your own thing. Old rules and traditions are suspect, if not to be discarded.

The expansion clubs of the early sixties, the Angels, the Colt .45s, and the Mets, added deep pockets and greater demand for ballplayers. The older, established clubs didn't want to relinquish any control, especially over salaries and bonuses. However, they couldn't keep the genie in the bottle.

In early 1964 Hughie's eyes blinked with the news that Rick Reichardt, an outfielder with the University of Wisconsin, signed with the Angels for an eye-popping $205,000 bonus. How could any owner spend that kind of money on an untested college kid? Clubs would go broke paying bonuses. It was like betting against the house.

The owners were determined to put a clamp on bonuses. They feared the consequences. They also wanted clubs other than the Yankees, Dodgers, Giants, and Cardinals to have a chance to win the league pennants and World Series. Thrown out was entrepreneurial scouting, in which one man used all his persuasive skills to sign a player; in its place was put an amateur draft system in which initially only one club negotiated with a player, no matter who found him. The siren song of parity led the rush to "Making Way for Tomorrow."

In June 1965 the owners adopted the draft system. It immediately stood on center stage under a blaring light, untested and already under suspicion as an opaque policy to control bonuses.

The owners thought that a draft system would keep bonuses down, as only one club could go after a player, not a half dozen, all clamoring to sign a hot prospect. It never happened. Within the next ten years, the baseball owners found themselves on the defensive again. The pendulum swung over to favor the players, with their increasing powerful players association.

Hughie's thirty years in baseball turned upside-down with the news about the draft system. The rules he had accepted as gospel no longer applied. Scouting took a sharp turn toward the political left.

The draft was designed to make clubs equal. As with the federal government's War on Poverty, the redistribution of wealth became the goal. Every new policy has tradeoffs. If the draft was to control players' bonuses and to give also-ran clubs a chance to be pennant contenders, it was successful. For scouts of the old school, it was a disaster.

Before the draft Hughie could cajole and persuade a kid's parents or his young wife. "Sign the contract now. You never know what the next guy will offer, if, in fact, anyone else will offer anything."

The good old days disappeared. Now every scout put names into the pot—a pot of common knowledge, swirled and shaken, blended and homogenized. But when clubs began sipping at the results, whose evaluation could they trust? Did another scout's opinion really account for what made a kid's heart tick when he ran onto the ball field?

Socialized scouting was in. It had been a good run for almost forty years, but the draft took the challenge and the skill out of scouting. Everybody's evaluation of the next Sandy Koufax or Hank Aaron or Mickey Mantle became communal property. Every scout knew what every other scout was doing and how he rated each prospect.

For Hughie, scouting's fabric, its strength, was torn, irreparable.

He needed to find another job in baseball, maybe negotiating trades. He knew that he could survive, but he needed a crash course in BND —that is, Building a New Dream.

Hughie grew mellow and his eyes glanced downward as he got to this point in his story. "Danny, I probably shouldn't talk about it. My friends in scouting might get upset. But everything I learned in scouting was gone. I learned to keep my players' evaluations a secret. I didn't even want other scouts to know who I was looking at, unless it was to benefit my club.

"Now everything is made public. All these scouting reports pooled into one big pot. How would anybody know about a prospect if he didn't know much, if anything, about the scouts doing the reporting? Then they stirred all that information into a big pot. So what do you get? If you're talking about hundreds of thousands of dollars, who knows what you're getting."

Hughie shrugged his shoulders thirty years later, thinking about the good old days. "Yes, those times were good for me," he observed.

Before 1965 someone had asked, "How are things going?"

"They're going good. I'm making some good deals and the players are getting great bonuses."

After 1965, things got tougher.

"How are things going?"

"Not good, no good. Scouting has lost its roots. Now it's socialized."

He loved the brotherhood of scouts. The work bred camaraderie, like drinking a beer after a game with his toughest competitors but always keeping his tongue in a guarded mode. He loved "salting the mine" with stories about nonexistent stars on an American Legion team two hundred miles away. Just watching a lazy competitor's brow wrinkle as he subtly asked for more information tugged at Hughie's ego. Yes, secrecy was a key asset of a scout, mixed occasionally with trickery.

He prized and guarded his contacts, or tipsters, that took years to develop. Quid pro quo, to use the language of lawyers and politicians —ask for favors and discreetly give favors.

Wondering initially if he should leave scouting, Hughie then decided to hang in there a little longer. He would try, but his heart wasn't in it. Maybe the Major Leagues would abolish the draft after a few years. Hughie wanted things to stay the same, but everything would have to change to return to another era. "Let scouts use their own wiles to find the talent," he cajoled.

For all his successes, the future appeared bleak. Surely the baseball owners and commissioner, in their wisdom, would pick up the torn fabric of baseball and mend it. It didn't happen. What Hughie keenly felt was that unknown changes were thrust upon him, pushing out old, accustomed ways of doing business. Would these new ways bring something of value in place of the draft system?

It was not just the draft system that rattled the foundations of baseball. From the exodus of the Giants and Dodgers to the West Coast in the late fifties to the end of the unconditional reserve clause in 1975, Hughie's baseball universe took a hit of 9.0 on the Richter scale. However, the rumblings did not stop. They remained with him for the rest of his career. Strikes, work stoppages, drugs, agents, and the internationalization of the game tested his resilience and love for baseball.

Devoted to always making a deal, Hughie now faced some hard questions about his future. In the midst of unprecedented changes, it is easy to talk about the past and ponder the future in a hotel bar. As he recalled from his days on the farm, everybody talked about the weather last year and next week. But a lingering paralysis entered conversations about what would happen today.

The same shrug of the shoulders affected baseball. What did all these changes mean? Hughie knew what was occurring to the game, but how would his job change? He would soon find out.

"Campanis, I gotta get out. It's just a question of time, and either you're gonna make me a big league scout, or I'm goin' with somebody who will," he complained to Al.

And he meant what he said. He wasn't belligerent to his boss, because he didn't think that was right. Campanis said he would take care of him.

"By God, if you don't, I'll leave," he replied emphatically.

Hughie believed that sitting down with a young man and his family to discuss his professional baseball career was the fit and proper way. It was time-honored and steeped in baseball traditions. Friendly persuasion—that's what Hughie had. And he knew that no one was better at twisting arms than he. With his Oklahoma twang, he made people comfortable. He knew his people. He knew what stories to tell that no easterner or Southern Californian could understand.

What did not change for Hughie were the twins named Judgment and Lady Luck.

Hughie, always mindful of Branch Rickey's admonition about infield stability, became a party to the longest stable infield in the modern era. Ron Cey at third, Bill Russell at shortstop, Davey Lopes at second, and Steve Garvey at first. They stayed together for eight years (1974–81), well ahead of several clubs with five years, including the Cubs' Frank Chance, Johnny Evers, Joe Tinker, and Harry Steinfeldt combination of 1906–10.

Bill Russell hailed from Pittsburg, Kansas. He played basketball; his high school was too small to field a baseball team. Hughie heard about him from a reliable coach who thought he had the tools to make the Major Leagues. What he lacked in experience could be developed in the Minor Leagues in a few years. Hughie recommended that the Dodgers draft Russell, which they did in 1966.

After four years in the Minors Russell packed his bags and headed to Chavez Ravine. He played the outfield until 1970, when Walter Alston moved him to shortstop to replace Maury Wills. A respectable infielder, although sometimes prone to making too many errors, Russell played longer with the Dodgers than any other player except Zack Wheat.

Davey Lopes traveled from his birthplace in Rhode Island to attend Washburn University in Topeka, Kansas, where his baseball team won an NAIA title. Initially drafted by the Giants in 1967, he became a Dodger a year later by being drafted a second time.

He spent five years in the Minors, finally coming to the Dodgers in 1973 as an outfielder and second baseman. During the following year he switched to second base full time. Strong in the field, he also stole bases regularly, even stealing twenty-five bases at age forty.

From the 1974 season to 1981, this infield quartet anchored a strong defensive team that won four NL pennants and one World Series title. They also remained the infield that played together the longest in MLB history. Rickey was right. A winning club needs a stable infield.

19

Building a New Dream

The word hit the Alexander family in Oklahoma City like an oil gusher. Uncle Hughie was leaving the Dodgers and moving to the Phillies. Nobody could believe it. Pam, his niece, was heartbroken.

"Uncle Hugh, why are you leaving the Dodgers, a club with a colorful history, a top team winning NL pennants and World Series? And now you're going to a club at the bottom rung of the Major Leagues. I can't believe you're doing this," she lamented.

Hughie offered a quick reply. "The reason I'm going to the Phillies is that it's a good organization and they gave me the opportunity to build this franchise from the bottom up. They have enough money to allow us to go out and build a first-class team. I guarantee you, Pam, that we will build a first-class team and we will win the World Series."

It was time for Hughie to turn another baseball page. The Phillies had some hot prospects waiting for a chance to become stars. Over the past couple of years they had signed their picks in the amateur draft to get back on their feet. With Hughie's own determination and drive, the Phillies would eventually win a World Series title.

And they did it in 1980. When Pam and other relatives traveled to Kansas City to see a World Series game, Hughie's first words were, "Well, I told you we would play in the World Series, and we're going to win it." And the Phillies did.

Going with the Phillies in the winter of 1971 as a Major League scout was also the biggest change in Hughie's career, propelled by events far outside his control. Labor strife, the end of the unconditional reserve clause by the mid-1970s, the beginning of free agency, and the amateur draft system, by then in its sixth year, reverberated throughout baseball's scouting circles.

He remained quietly opposed to the Major League draft system, because scouting just wasn't the same. He kept sticking it out because he thought that the owners might return to the old system. But after five years of waiting, Hughie finally realized that baseball owners were keeping it. If he was going to change jobs, he had to know somebody with the right contacts.

Paul Owens, a longtime friend, had joined the Phillies in the mid-1960s as its general manager. He and Hughie saw one another around National League parks, looking at players for their clubs (and occasionally were at odds with one another, chasing the same players). At a ballpark in 1970, Hughie spotted Paul.

"Let's go out and have a drink, Hughie," Paul offered.

Hughie quickly accepted.

Within an hour, Paul flatly told Hughie, "Damn, I need you in Philly with me, Hughie. I need you in the worst way."

"Well, dammit, if you can pay me enough money. I don't make a lot, but I make a helluva lot more than your club pays," Hughie replied.

"How much do you make?" Owens asked.

"$15,000," Hughie replied.

"Oh, Jesus, the highest-paid scout I got is about $12,000," Paul answered.

Later, during the early summer of 1971, Paul and Hughie met again in Atlanta, both of them looking at a number-one draft pick who had played for the Padres. After an afternoon game they met for a long evening dinner. Owens finally said he'd see if he could get Hughie the $15,000.

The next morning they had breakfast, and Hughie asked Paul if he remembered what he said the previous night. "Yeah," Owens answered.

Back in Philly the next day, Paul talked with Bob Carpenter about Hughie. Paul had already begun a revamping of the Phillies organization a few years earlier. He strengthened its farm club system by hiring Dallas Green. Green had signed some top-notch players in the amateur draft. Now Owens began hiring scouts, putting together major changes in player development and scouting. (Before Owens's arrival, the Phillies front office had talked a lot about changes, but nothing was done.)

Owens was a smart guy who made decisions. He knew if he didn't make any decisions, the Phillies would remain drifting in or near last place, as they had for the past several years. To put his plan together, he needed Hughie to work with Dallas on the fine points of scouting and signing players in the amateur draft and to help him make trades.

A couple of months later Paul called Hughie and asked if he still would come over and help him. Hughie said, "Yes, but I want to come to Philadelphia and sit down with you and the Carpenter family and everybody and we'll go over this. I've got to have certain things, but I have to be sure that I am doing the right thing." Hughie spoke with a healthy dose of bravado. With thirty-five years of scouting experience, he spoke about himself with assurance, driven by street smarts and intense motivation. Whatever deal he pursued, he injected it with a sense of urgency.

A week later Hughie arrived in Philadelphia to begin some serious talk about becoming a scout for them. He spent a day and a half with the two Carpenters, Paul Owens, and John Quinn, then the general manager. Finally, Ruly Carpenter asked if all the fellows were through with Hughie. They all said yes.

Ruly said, "I want to ask you a question." (Hughie knew something was on his mind because he kept tapping his foot during the meeting.) "Okay, here it is, Hughie."

"Shoot, go right ahead," Hughie answered.

"Why are the Dodgers so damn successful?"

"I can tell you that, Ruly, in about thirty seconds."

"Well, I want to hear it," Ruly retorted.

"I know your dad is sitting right here, and he has spent a lot of money on bonuses for ballplayers."

"That's right. We have a quota up here. We set aside $400,000 per year for bonuses for young players."

"Do you know what the Dodgers set aside every year for bonuses?"

"No, what?"

"$1 million, and if we run out of money, which we do almost every year, the Dodgers throw in another $100,000 or so when we got a good ballplayer that we are trying to keep out of college. We go to the boss and say we need some more money. We would get another $100,000 or so. We always spend about $1.2 million. And I say we sign 50, 60, or 70. One year we signed 108 players."

They just couldn't get over that, because their policy was to sign about fifteen or twenty players.

Furthermore, Hughie continued, "You can't compete when you're signing fifteen or twenty players and we're signing a hundred. You can't beat it, ain't no way, 'cause a lot of players that we sign are not going to play in the big leagues. You sign 'em with a question mark. After about a year, you say, 'Oh, he's goin' to make it now.'"

"So that's what it is," Ruly said.

Hughie took the initiative. "If you're going to bring me over here, then Paul Owens and I are gonna' run it, and if you put a clamp on us, I'll quit. I won't take the job, I'll quit."

The years of suffering in Philadelphia dogged everybody. Hughie, he didn't have time to dwell in the past. You gotta move on *with a plan*. The words resounded in his mind.

There was a long silence. Ruly nodded his head affirmatively.

"Yes, I'll take the job," Hughie quickly replied.

The divide between what the Phillies were and what they could become was immense. That was the challenge.

Within days of leaving the Dodgers, Hughie found himself help-ing his new club organize its own thinking. With Owens focusing on player development, a beefed-up scouting system, and trades that meant giving up some hot prospects in their Minor Leagues to get the veteran players to become a pennant contender, Hughie and everybody else knew it would not be done in two or three years.

Two of Hughie's first jobs were to work directly with Dallas to teach him the ABCs of amateur scouting and to help Paul Owens with trades. It was his job to sit down and decide which trades made sense. Then he had to explain it and, in some cases, persuade his boss. But that's what he got paid for—persuading those less inclined to make radical changes in a club quickly.

"Dallas," Hughie offered, "you have to break the player down. Then you won't make big mistakes. Remember to find what tools of the trade a player has. Rare is the discovery of a player with all five tools of the trade. If a player has three of them, he has an excellent chance to make baseball a career. It's the mechanics that you look for, and don't get hypnotized by a guy's performance."

Both Hughie and Dallas also knew that the biggest question mark about a player is his courage and heart. Does he hustle? If he has a bad day, does the feeling carry over to the next game? A good player has both a short-term and a long-term memory. A short one for making an error or striking out, a long one for remembering the mechanics of sound batting, fielding, and throwing. When a kid combines those traits, he begins to acquire baseball intelligence.

When not attending to his work with Green, Paul sent Hughie out on the road to evaluate the players the Phillies wanted. For thirty-six years Hughie had played and worked with winning clubs. Now working for the Phillies was to be his biggest challenge. However, his mindset, his canny judgment of talent, and a rolodex of contacts in both leagues became his own tools of the trade.

Quickly Hughie observed that Veterans Stadium, with its Astro-turf playing surface, called for speed and quickness. Speed in the outfield to snag balls skipping like tennis balls, quickness to accelerate immediately. The Phillies needed both skills.

Nobody wanted to play for the Phillies. With the team having resided in the bottom half of the standings for nearly a decade, the spectators' raucous, obnoxious behavior had taken a toll on players' morale. Philadelphia's label as the City of Brotherly Love didn't apply once "fans" entered Shibe Park or Veterans Stadium. There's a story about when the Phillies played in Shibe Park back in the thirties, and the fence was adorned by an advertisement for soap, "The Phillies Use Lifebuoy." Some fans retorted, "They still stink." That image hadn't changed by the late sixties and early seventies.

20

Let's Get Real about Rebuilding This Club

The Phillies had come off four consecutive losing seasons, and the 1972 season was to be no exception. Their last winning season was in 1964, when they blew a six-and-a-half-game lead with twelve games remaining with the Cardinals, clinching the pennant by one game. The remainder of the decade was spent in second division.

The 1972 season was a disaster. They won fifty-nine and lost ninety-seven. Only the four-year-old expansion club the Padres did worse. Steve Carlton was the one redeeming light. He compiled an incredible 27-10 record that represented 45 percent of the Phillies' wins. He capped the year with the Cy Young Award and won the NL triple crown in pitching—ERA, strikeouts, and victories.

Carlton had come over to the Phillies (spring 1972) just before Hughie arrived in what has been described as the best (or worst) trade in baseball history, depending on whether one is a Cardinals or a Phillies fan. The Phillies had to give up Rick Wise, their hard-throwing right-hander anchor pitcher.

Hughie got a head's-up about the trade, although he was still with the Dodgers. "Augie Busch, the Cardinals owner, didn't like Carlton. Called him a pussy foot and Busch didn't want to pay him the $75,000 asking salary. So he told the front office to get rid of him. They didn't want to, but the boss ordered Carlton to be traded. Some clubs liked 'Lefty' and some others didn't, but the Phillies jumped at the chance. He had a great slider and had fine control," Hughie observed.

At least the '72 season witnessed at least one bright spot. The Phillies held a .981 fielding average, second highest in the NL, headlined by shortstop Larry Bowa, third baseman Don Money, and second baseman Denny Doyle. The pitching staff also had a respectable season's ERA of 3.66.

Obviously the hitting was anemic: a paltry .236 with an OBP of .302 with only 503 runs scored during the entire season. Owens, Green, and Alexander had a major overhaul facing them to make the Phillies more competitive. Speed, relief pitching, and hitting—getting two of the three without giving up their core defensive players and emerging stars from the farm clubs would tax any street-smart guys.

The Phillies had to make some off-season deals. It would involve giving up some good ballplayers in their farm club pipeline. They had a lot of success in signing players in the amateur draft. In 1968 they signed Greg Luzinski in the first round. Three years later they picked Roy Thomas, a right-handed pitcher, in the first round and Mike Schmidt in the second round. Alan Bannister became the first-round draft pick in 1973, widely acclaimed among college players for his versatility in the outfield and infield.

Also in the farm system, Larry Bowa and Denny Doyle, weak hitters but superb infielders and fierce competitors, made the switch to the big leagues quickly. In quick succession in the following two years they signed Larry Christenson, a right-handed pitcher; John Stearns, catcher; Dick Ruthven, pitcher; and Lonnie Smith, outfielder.

Mike Schmidt and Greg Luzinski had made the Phillies' roster in Hughie's first year. These players became the core of a makeover of the Phillies, along with Steve Carlton, Larry Bowa, Tim McCarver, Bob Boone, Larry Christenson, Lonnie Smith, and Tom Hutton for the remainder of the decade.

Within weeks after the '72 season, Owens and Hughie began making trades to rebuild the club. Now the tough part—getting other clubs that had some players the Phillies needed to come to the bargaining table. The requirement—being a gutsy poker player with the finesse of a diplomat in going for the quick fix but not giving away the young talent coming up from the Minors. It is always a trade-off, a balancing act between getting the veterans and keeping the promising young players. Besides, Dallas Green would not be happy to see a lot of his Minor League prospects traded.

Hughie remembered what Branch Rickey observed, that the best trade is when both clubs are winners. Frank Lane and Paul Richards reaffirmed the idea. The players traded did a good job with their new clubs. At least, the key players did. That's what Hughie wanted, because then he could always come back to the general manager knowing that his word could be trusted. It makes for good trading, and your reputation gets out around the league.

In late October '72, in an effort to rebuild the Phillies' pitching corps, Paul and Hughie traded Don Money, John Vukovich, and Billy Champion to Milwaukee (then in the AL) for pitchers Jim Lonborg, Ken Sanders, Ken Brett, and Earl Stephenson. Now they had to go after relief pitchers and speed in the outfield.

After the '72 season Danny Ozark, a longtime fixture of the Dodger organization, became the Phillies' manager, replacing Frank Lucchesi. Hughie had worked with Danny when he managed some Dodger farm clubs and later became a coach for Walter Alston. An easygoing man, Ozark had the experience and personality to develop a winning chemistry.

Everybody needs a mentor, someone who believes in you and will be brutally honest about your abilities. Fortunate is the player who pairs up with a mentor, whether he is twenty years old or even forty. Hughie had a double dose of mentoring from two godfathers of baseball—Cy Slapnicka and Branch Rickey.

Although neither one ever mentioned any indebtedness Hughie owed to up-and-coming scouts, Slapnicka and Rickey expected Hughie to follow in their footsteps. Teach a new generation of young men about scouting. In the last thirty years of his career he had taught a lot of guys about finding and judging talent. He opened the doors to them because he thought they loved the game and had the talent and discipline to be successful.

One was Doug Gassaway, whom Hughie signed as a player in 1959 or 1960. Doug had hung around the Minor Leagues for eleven years, ending up pitching the last three in the Mexican League. Hanging up his spikes, he returned to the Fort Worth area and began umpiring. They lost contact with one another until the early seventies.

Hughie was scouting a game in Fort Worth with a couple of other guys when he remarked, "Damn, I know that umpire behind home plate. But I can't tell you exactly who he is."

Hughie sent a message to him after the game. It was Doug Gassaway. "Let's meet at my hotel and talk."

Doug had a drive-through grocery store in nearby Arlington and umpired college and high school games on the side. However, he missed the game, so Hughie told him to meet at the ballpark the next day. "We'll talk about scouting."

The next several days they met at some ballparks. Hughie broke down different players—their running, throwing, hitting, fielding, and, yes, hustling. Every day they went over some parts of the game. After Hughie left town, they got together on the phone.

Doug was a quick learner. If he made a mistake, he didn't make it a second time.

"Yeah, you're gonna make some mistakes. That's the way you learn." Part of Hughie's disarming manner was his belief that if a scout never makes a mistake, then he is afraid of making a decision about a prospect. It's like fielding a ball. If the player never touches the ball, then there is no error.

"That's the way you learn," Hughie repeated. "Now, if you listen and don't become bullheaded, I'll teach you not to make the same mistakes again and again. If you don't follow my advice, then you'll be too costly to your club, and you're out of the game."

Within a few weeks Doug took over part of Hughie's territory for the Phillies. They remained in touch with one another for the rest of Hughie's life, trading stories and advice, but Hughie would not make Doug's decisions. Doug had to make things happen, not just watch things happen.

Hughie took on a godfather's role. He became a rock-roller, helping neophytes transform themselves from those who watched and wondered what was happening to those who made things happen. Accountability was always in their laps.

He helped a lot of "wannabe" scouts, but he wasn't going to do their work. In his book, the word *helping* meant getting the guy to make plans. Hughie would open some doors, but there would be no pushing a rookie through it.

Hughie kept in contact with many of his fellow scouts and adversaries. Now he was the veteran, not a rookie. At a ballpark or in a hotel room, he cajoled and jawboned, trying to get his viewpoint across. One night he got into a heated argument, albeit a friendly one, with another scout about Rickey's ideas. They argued all night long, just eggin' each other on.

"You old son of a bitch! How many players have you got in the big leagues, right now, at this moment? I've got about fifteen or twenty playing in the big leagues right now, and you got two. I got ahead of you by signing quantity and not all quality," boasted Hughie.

21

Trading Who, and Trading When

Negotiating trades can give you a big rush or a gigantic letdown. Sometimes they are conducted in a business-like manner with several executives huddling around a table, then adjourning to separate rooms to make a decision. Other times you have a few drinks in a bar with guys at winter meetings and, after a few hours of partying, you make a trade. Whatever the chemistry of a trade, it is followed by another seventy-two hours of suspense, wondering if someone will back out at the last second.

Fortunately, insider trading is legal in baseball, if not on Wall Street. At least, no one has ever been charged with a felony. It is simply an acceptable part of the game, like "stealing" signs during a game or pretending to be hit by a pitched ball.

To pull off the deals they wanted, Paul and Hughie worked all their contacts developed over the years. They knew that baseball is a zero-sum game. Victories determine one's fate, despite looking to the future for players to make the club a pennant contender. They developed and then followed a methodical, disciplined plan to get the players they needed to get them there as fast as possible. During the next four years the Phillies made key acquisitions by getting speedy Bake McBride and relievers Tug McGraw and Ron Reed. Fortunately, Larry Christenson joined the club at age nineteen in 1973 as a starter helping Carlton. Christenson, a first-draft selection in June 1972, matured quickly. By 1977 he hurled a sparkling 19-6 record, winning fifteen of his last sixteen games.

In late 1973 the Phillies tried to land pitcher Ron Schueler from the Braves. The Braves wanted pitcher Randy Lerch, the Phillies' good left-hander in exchange. But a Braves official got Lerch mixed up with Barry Lersch, a right-handed pitcher. According to *Baseball Digest*, a Braves executive found out the error when he called Lersch: "Lefty, we're glad to have you." Lersch responded, "I'm a righty." The trade included medicinal doses of silence and embarrassment in Atlanta.

Randy Lerch, a good-hitting starting pitcher, became a mainstay with the Phillies, enjoying three double-figure seasons in his eleven years with the Phillies.

The second big trade was getting Tug McGraw a year later (December 1974) from the Mets. A flaky, left-handed reliever, McGraw coined the "You Gotta Believe" rallying cry for the Mets' pennant drive in 1973. "What a helluva trade!" Hughie thought. The Mets had McGraw up for trade because he had pitched for them for nine years and supposedly had a bad back. Hughie spotted an opportunity to have a lefty reliever who could close a game.

Hughie told Paul just after the '74 season about the possibility of getting McGraw. (Dallas was in New Orleans in a player meeting and so was not involved in the discussion.) "We'll just go to the Mets and see if we can trade for McGraw."

They got up in the hotel room and the Mets had about five or six people there discussing as many as eight players. Finally, after about four or five hours, the Mets said that they would make the trade but they wanted John Stearns and two other players, Del Unser and Mac Scarce.

Stearns was a tough catcher and a go-getter who played baseball the way he had played football at the University of Colorado, tough and aggressive. Boy, that was a helluva decision, because Stearns was the Phillies' best prospect in their entire farm club system. In the club's favor, they had two veteran catchers, Bob Boone and Tim McCarver.

"Paul, what do you think?" Hughie asked.

"Damn, I don't know. Dallas will kill both of us."

"The hell with Dallas Green! If we don't get McGraw, we can't win! There's no way we can win without a reliever. Let's go ahead and make the damn trade. The hell with it! We're backed with catchers. We're all right!" Hughie spoke with confidence.

They returned to the room and made the trade. In subsequent years Tug McGraw paid big dividends. He was the closer the Phillies needed. Farm director Dallas Green really got ticked off at Hughie and Paul, though, because they were trading his young players coming through the Minor Leagues, the guys he loved. However, Paul and Hughie were not going to halt the rebuilding of the club just to protect Dallas's top prospects.

Player development and trading invite strong disagreements. It is inevitable when trying to make the right deals to get veteran players, especially as the club had a great farm system by the early seventies. With Paul and Hughie always having an inkling about who they could get from other clubs, they looked at their Minor League prospects as trump cards.

Dallas had imbued their farm clubs with the methods to prepare players to play the "Phillies Way." Specific instructions were sent to each club. All Minor League players knew what the Phillies were doing, and they practiced their thought processes unmercifully in different baseball situations. If these young kids were to make it to the Big Show, they had to learn the fundamentals in the Minor Leagues, not at Veterans Stadium. Phillies fans had little tolerance for players learning the game in a Major League uniform.

After two last-place finishes in the NL East in '72 and '73, the club improved to a third-place, 80-82 record in '74. In '75 they climbed above the .500 mark with a second-place, 86-76 season. The trades paid off. Their offense improved while the defense remained in peak form.

The years 1974 and '75 brought a seismic upheaval in baseball. In December 1974 Catfish Hunter got his release from Charles Finley of the Oakland A's. Within a few days Peter Seitz, a federal arbitrator, ruled that if a club did not sign its ballplayer within a year, there was no contractual bond between the player and the club. A player was free to negotiate with any Major League club.

A year later Seitz ruled in the cases of Andy Messersmith and Dave McNally that they were free agents. The reserve clause became nothing more than a one-year option. The pendulum of power swung swiftly over to the players. The owners had simply waited too long, thinking that the status quo would remain untouched, like the Supreme Court's decision in the 1920s exempting baseball from antitrust legislation.

Speculation among club owners, agents, players, and sports writers about the economic impact of the end of the reserve clause filled hours of conversations and thousands of column inches. Would the rich clubs dominate both leagues again? How could poorer clubs in secondary TV markets compete? No one had answers.

Meanwhile, Hughie, Paul, and Dallas pressed forward on player development and trades. With a modified reserve system, there were no longer any long-term guarantees. If the Phillies could not compete in multimillion-dollar contracts, they had no option but to build a winning club by trading. No longer could a club sign one hundred rookies with the hope that seven would make it to the big leagues.

The trio figured that the Phillies needed three or four more players to make it to the playoffs, so they decided to trade some of their good players within the farm system. They kept it a secret, made the trade, and then called Danny Ozark, the new manager. "We got you so-and-so ballplayer, Danny."

At the end of the '75 season three more top amateur picks—Dick Ruthven, Roy Thomas, and Alan Bannister—packed their bags for Comiskey Park. Also coming to the Phillies were lefty pitcher Jim Kaat and rookie shortstop Mike Buskey.

The Phillies were set to go after the NL flag after a quarter-century drought.

Sometimes you help a friend. Hughie had known Ron Clark from his scouting days with the Dodgers, and they enjoyed a camaraderie built on similar backgrounds. Clark grew up in Fort Worth, spent a lot of time as a kid around the rodeo circuit, and finally joined the Twins in the mid-1960s. By 1975 he needed just a couple of months to get a full pension. Hughie got him that chance, and Clark stayed the following year as a coach. He also assisted Dallas Green in player development by evaluating the Phillies' Minor League players.

An axiom worth repeating: the best clubs always have the best scout and the best farm clubs. Then the parent club has the flexibility to trade players for other players, or cash.

Ron knew how to judge pitchers and delivered daily and weekly reports to Dallas, Paul, and Hughie. He elaborated at great length about a pitcher's delivery and command—that is, his ability to throw the ball at both sides of the plate. Good delivery is made with a loose arm, and it's easy to spot a kid "muscling" the ball by squeezing it too tight or twisting his wrist on delivery.

He spent a lot of time with pitchers, figuring it was easier to teach pitchers how to pitch than it was to teach hitters how to hit. No manager in baseball ever boasted about having too many good pitchers.

Hughie and Dallas thought Ron had the potential to be a manager, and three years later, in 1979, he managed the Spartanburg, South Carolina, farm club, moving to Reading, Pennsylvania, the next year. A few months into the 1980 season Ron sent a report about a rookie named Ryne Sandberg, whom the Phillies had drafted in 1978. "Sandberg is an above average runner, can steal bases at the Major League level. His arm is below average with a slow release of the ball. At the Major League level, second base is best. Good power to the opposite field, can hit into the gap. A smart player, low key, and quiet."

Sandberg made his Major League debut two years later, landing himself on a World Series championship team. Within a year he packed his bags with Larry Bowa to head west to the Cubs, both teaming up with Dallas again, who had accepted the job as the Cubs' general manager.

Hughie's reputation among the general managers of the other National League clubs for making a square deal with his word and a handshake paid big dividends during the seventies. In the sixties he and Bing Devine of the Cardinals had talked baseball. Devine had given Hughie some pointers about the intricacies of player development and the art of making trades.

When Devine returned to the Cardinals, Hughie renewed their old friendship. It resulted in the Phillies getting Tim McCarver again, who had played with them in '70 and '71. Just after the '75 season began, McCarver returned to the Phillies, as Carlton wanted him as his personal catcher. (Carlton broke in as a rookie with McCarver as the Cardinal catcher.)

In late 1975 Paul and Hughie got another fine right-handed reliever when they traded Mike Anderson, a number-one draft pick, to the Cardinals for Ron Reed. Now they had a winning lefty-righty duo in the bullpen, Reed and McGraw. It paid dividends for the next eight years, as the trades with the Cardinals were built on years of solid friendship and respect between Hughie and Bing.

Nothing deterred Hughie if he wanted a certain player. He knew everybody. If a player he sought was unhappy with a club, he knew about it as quickly as the player's general manager, if not sooner. With his booming voice and ever-present smile, people just opened up to him.

With a drink in his hand or a deck of cards, he opened his mouth and out popped a flood of profanity. No one thought about it. It was just Uncle Hughie, with an Oklahoma twang and wide smile.

Beneath the surface lay a defiant Hugh Alexander. No one would get a player he wanted. He cajoled, he laughed, and he appealed to a player's higher instincts. A player just didn't say no to his face. It would be sacrilegious. Just playing ball with Hughie's team was a gift.

If the Phillies were to get to the playoffs, they needed more power hitting, so they traded for Richie Allen. The White Sox wanted to unload Allen, ever temperamental, so they traded him to the Braves in 1975. Before playing one game with the Braves, the Phillies picked up his contract and gave the Braves Barry Bonnell, Jim Essian, and cash.

Allen began his Major League career with the Phillies in 1963 wrapping up the NL Rookie of the Year Award, but by 1969 he had worn out his welcome through his off-field theatrics. He was traded to the Cardinals and eventually returned to Philadelphia in early '75, after stops in Chicago (White Sox) and Atlanta. Despite his reputation, Hughie thought Allen's power would bring a pennant. It did not happen.

Everybody wanted more foot speed, especially as Astroturf replaced grass in many National League parks. Unlike the other tools of the trade, speed cannot be taught. A player has it or he doesn't. They went after outfielder Garry Maddox of the Giants and gave up Willie Montanez in the spring of '75. Maddox compensated for the slow-footed left fielder Greg Luzinski. For the next eight years Maddox won the Gold Glove Award.

Getting Maddox was a godsend. The trade developed slowly, as a longtime friend of Hughie's, Fred Goodman, flew out to the West Coast to look at the left-handed pitcher Ron Bryant. Goodman reported that Bryant was out of shape and didn't throw that well, although in '73 he led the league in wins with a 24-12 record. But a diving-board accident left Bryant with a back injury, and in the following year he slumped to a 3-15 record.

Goodman found out while scouting Bryant that Wes Westrum, the Giants manager, didn't like Maddox and wanted to get rid of him. Goodman called Hughie. "You need to come out here to take a look at Maddox."

After a couple of days at the Giants park, both agreed that he was a promising player and ready to come to the big leagues to stay. Another thing that impressed them was that Maddox "got off" at the crack of the bat.

Outfielders and infielders needed that kind of quickness. They recommended to Paul Owens a deal with Westrum, swapping Willie Montanez, a first baseman and outfielder who was having some knee problems, in an even trade with Maddox. It was a done deal.

Hughie heard a rumor in the early part of the '77 season that Bake

McBride was up for trade by the Cardinals. So he called Owens, who told Hughie to get to St. Louis immediately to talk with Bing Devine. "Take a look at him and see if his knees are okay," Paul ordered.

Bing and Hughie had known one another for several years during Bing's on-again, off-again tenure as general manager of the Cardinals. (In 1972 Augie Busch ordered Devine to trade Steve Carlton to the Phillies for Rick Wise, just at the time that Carlton was reaching his prime.)

The health reports circulating among the clubs said that McBride had two bad knees. Even after some operations, they remained stiff. So Hughie stayed in St. Louis for about six days to watch him and talk with Devine about a trade. McBride looked all right. But the club was taking a helluva a gamble. Hughie hopped a plane to Cincinnati, where Owens was with the club, to talk about McBride's knees with the team doctor and another specialist.

For thirty-eight hours in a hotel room, the Phillies staff discussed McBride. Finally, Hughie got had the idea to leave the two docs together without others present and let them decide. He figured that the docs would not lie to one another. They might not give out a lot of information, but they wouldn't tell one another a bare-ass lie.

The Phillies finally traded for McBride in June, but they had to give up some good talent. Dallas threw a fit. He said he was going to quit, because the players Hughie traded to the Cardinals were left-handed pitcher Tom Underwood, along with Rick Bosetti and Dane Iorg.

"Dammit, Chief [Hughie's affectionate nickname for Green], we didn't give up any ballplayer. We gave up a little left-handed pitcher that you liked so damn much who ain't going to pitch very good in the big leagues, if he ever pitches, and we gave up a Minor League outfielder who can run. But he's never played in the big leagues. We gave up two players, and we'll get a better one," Hughie argued. (A year after the McBride trade, Devine was fired again by the Cardinals and for a couple of years came over to the Phillies as a scout.)

Four years after the disastrous '72 season, the Phillies posted a 101-61 record in '76, the first time in the club's history that it won more than one hundred games in a season, finishing first in the NL East. They scored 770 runs, an increase of 267 over the '72 club. Their .272 team batting average was 36 points higher and their .981 fielding average was identical to 1972. Their game plan worked.

Although they lost the NL Championship Series to Cincinnati's Big Red Machine, they celebrated the bicentennial with the rest of the nation. "Wait 'til next year!"

The '77 Phillies duplicated the preceding year's record, 101-61, with superb defense and speed and a 344-run differential over the '72 club. Again they lost in the NL Championship Series, this time to the Dodgers.

Lesser people would have been at one another's throat years before with the trading of top amateur picks. Sportswriters, hearing a death knell, would have gathered around the funeral pyre speculating about who would be the first to resign or be fired. The rumor mill was churning in Philadelphia, but the Phillies' successes in the late '70s got in their way.

What Dallas, Hughie, and Paul had was a special recipe rarely found in a club. They trusted one another. No one could drive a wedge between them. They stuck together.

The media tried to do it.

The agents tried to do it.

The players tried to do it.

What stopped them was that Paul, Dallas, and Hughie believed in one another, because they had a game plan. They knew what was needed, whether a reliever, an outfielder, or a catcher. And if they had to trade some top draft picks to get those players, they did it. The three men became defined by what they did, not by what they had to do.

Scouting new talents and making new trades are the everyday grist of a ball club. As someone told Hughie, "Trading is like conducting a garage sale. I'll give you what I have in the bullpen for what you have in the dugout." All these efforts, usually concealed from the public by consenting adults, attract the attention of fans, baseball writers, and other clubs. The result: the club sells more tickets.

Time will tell if a trade is right. That's the trading business. Most front office executives want instant results. That's the American dream. Hughie knew that any good trade took time for a payoff. That same attitude helped Hughie when he was a carney.

In all his scouting years, he got on the fence with a lot of players. He'd see some have good days and then have really bad days. When he got on the fence with a player, he learned to say, "Hold it."

Hughie gave that advice to a lot of scouts he broke in. "You get on the fence, then walk away, and you will be right. If you're not careful, you'll forget about the little things he can't do real well, and that's a helluva mistake," Hughie said over and over.

22

You Can Lose If You Don't Know the Rules

Signing Marty Bystrom created a firestorm, and after the Phillies got him, baseball owners and the commissioner huddled together to change a rule. In early November 1976 Hughie got a call from newly hired Fred Goodman, who had just moved to Florida after a stint as a scout with the Oakland A's. "Hughie, there's a fine young pitcher by the name of Marty Bystrom out of Miami-Dade Community College," Fred remarked.

Paul DuVall, an area scout for the Phillies, and "Catfish" Smith, a part-time scout, had spotted him. He had good delivery and command, a rising fastball, and a good curve. He was a big kid, about six feet five, and strong.

DuVall had sent in a report about Bystrom and recommended that the Phillies draft him in January with a signing bonus of $40,000. (In those days the Major League clubs held two drafts a year, one in January and another in June.)

Fred asked Paul if Marty was drafted in June. The answer was no. Then Fred explained the interpretation of the rule that a club could sign a player who was in the June draft but not selected up to two weeks prior to the January draft.

Paul Owens called Dallas and told him about Marty's status. Exercising caution, Dallas wanted confirmation about the draft rule, so

Paul told him to call Fred Goodman. That night Dallas called Fred to ask him to explain the rule.

The rule: if a player is passed over in a junior college or high school amateur draft, he can be signed as a free agent. The player does not have to go through the draft again if his signing takes place at least two weeks prior to the next draft. Fred referred Dallas to a section in the Blue Book where he could find the rule. "Check it out with the commissioner's office, but don't mention the player's name. Just ask if a player can be signed as a free agent under that rule," Fred advised.

"Why don't we sign him now?" Hughie argued.

"Can't do that. He's in college and we're checking out the rule," Dallas snapped.

"Now keep in mind, the other clubs are going to cry 'foul' and 'unfair' when they hear about the deal, but there's nothing that they can do about it," continued Fred.

The next day Dallas called Fred again and told him that DuVall was going to arrange a workout for Bystrom. "I'm sending Hughie to watch him. Pick him up at the airport," Dallas ordered.

Before Hughie left for Miami, he called Catfish Smith to set up an appointment with the boy after the workout if the scouts liked what they saw. Bystrom was outstanding in the workout, and both Fred and Hughie recommended signing him.

Catfish didn't think it would do any good to try to convince Marty to sign, but Hughie remained defiant. He was not about to turn around and return to Philadelphia. About 10:30 p.m., they went over to Marty's home, but he was still working at a local gas station.

Just as they arrived, Marty's coach at Miami-Dade Community College showed up, angry and belligerent. Hughie had his hands full.

"I want to debate you here and now!" were the coach's first words.

"About what?" Hughie asked.

"Whether this boy ought to sign now or go to college one more year," snapped the coach.

"But I don't know anything about debating. I don't even know what the word means. I only went to school to the eleventh grade. I wouldn't even have a chance against you."

(Under his breath, Hughie said, "You son of a bitch. I'm going to debate you in about one hour, 'cause you're going to be in my field—baseball—and then I'm going to rub it in. You're not only rubbing me the wrong way, you're ridiculing me. Just wait. I'll get you. I'm going for the jugular.")

Until about 2:30 in the morning they debated. Hughie ate him alive. His old boxing days on the carnival circuit resurfaced, and he heard his father's words: "Lash out! Get aggressive. Throw the first, second, and third blows and don't stop until your opponent is flat down on the mat."

Within hours the coach headed out the door wondering if an Oklahoma tornado had hit him.

"Okay, offer him $50,000," Dallas said. "I want Hughie to sign the kid. He's the Major League scout." (Fred thought that the credit for signing should go to DuVall and Smith, but Dallas overruled him.)

The other clubs raised hell about the signing, but there was nothing that they could do about it. The rule was in the book, in black and white. The other club executives just didn't know about it. Sometimes ignorance has a steep price tag.

The next year the rule was changed about drafting players like Marty.

In September 1980 Marty joined the Phillies and in his first game shut out the Mets. By season's end he compiled a 5-0 record with a 1.50 ERA. In the World Series he started Game Five but left without a decision. He remained with the Phillies until 1984, when he was traded to the Yankees.

23

Finally a Winner

In '79 the Phillies took a tumble, hit hard with injuries. In September 1979 Danny Ozark was fired and Dallas took over the club as interim manager.

Paul Owens had tried to sign Pete Rose, a free agent, in December 1978 but didn't have the $500,000 to get him. He pressed the Carpenters to find the money. Finally, the deal was struck. Bill Giles, the Phillies' vice president of business, sold the radio and television rights to broadcast their games in early 1979 in order to pay Pete. Rose became the highest-paid athlete in all sports.

Rose became the catalyst for the Phillies. He was a unifier, a team player who came to the clubhouse and put aside what happened outside the ballpark. Baseball was his life. He knew how to play and what it took to win. A lot of players have the smarts to play the game well. Few learn to take the game a step higher—knowing how to win.

Hughie saw it coming. The Phillies could go to the World Series in 1980. Finally, for only the third time in Phillies history, they headed for the fall classic, this time against the Kansas City Royals. Behind Lefty's (Carlton), Tug's (McGraw), Marty's (Bystrom), and Ron's (Reed) pitching, they claimed their first World Series championship. It took Hughie, Dallas, and Paul eight years to win the World Series.

When the Series headed for Kansas City, Hughie met his niece and cousins at a hotel. "Well, I told you that the Phillies would win the pennant, and now they're going to win the World Series. Yep! That's what I told you." A smile that could melt a cold heart crossed his sun-bitten face.

They won the World Series by keeping their core players—Larry Bowa, Greg Luzinski, Mike Schmidt, Larry Christenson (all amateur draft picks), Bob Boone, Lonnie Smith, Tim McCarver, and Steve Carlton. Hughie's quiet yet outspoken manner paid off. People listened when Hughie spoke.

Hughie sat relaxing in an old leather chair behind his desk at Veterans Field after the World Series victory. There was a pile of scouting reports tempting him to look at another bunch of players, but he simply wanted to savor the moment. He had always worked for a winner. Finally the Phillies were on the winners' map.

A day later he began planning for the 1981 season. Ron Clark called to congratulate him and to remind him that the Double-A farm clubs in Spartanburg and Reading, Pennsylvania, had contributed to the victory. Ozzie Virgil Jr., catcher; Ryne Sandberg, infielder; Don Carman, pitcher; speedy Bobby Dernier, outfielder; and Mark Davis, reliever (a future Cy Young winner) played key roles.

A strong player development program with the best scouts and key personnel who know the rules—seemingly clichés—are essential for a winning combination. The Phillies demonstrated the truth of this axiom.

A new baseball dream came true. Three tough-minded guys, some boisterous crowds, and some independent-minded ballplayers all combined for a surreal moment. They trusted one another not just with a handshake but with a sense of responsibility and partnership. They left a good set of fingerprints on all the deals they made. That's the way baseball is supposed to be.

The 1981 season brought a player strike and a disappointing third-place finish for the Phillies. Everything was a mess. Then the Carpenter family, weary of escalating salaries, sold the club after thirty years of ownership to Bill Giles and others for $30 million.

Ruly Carpenter wondered aloud how he could keep the club afloat with two $100,000 players on the payroll. Then later he was quoted saying, "I'm going to write a book: *How to Make a Small Fortune in Baseball*. You start with a large fortune."

Success in baseball is often fleeting. The last time at bat is history; what counts now is the next pitch. Even last year's World Series hero is soon gone, traded to another team. The cast of characters changes unpredictably and quickly. Now, only one year after the Phillies won the World Series in 1980, Dallas Green called Hughie on the phone and said, "I've just been offered one helluva deal."

"What's that?" Hughie asked.

"What's that? I just have been offered the job of general manager of the Cubs. Dammit, it pays me $250,000!"

"Damn, that is a helluva deal. You were making $90,000 with the Phillies, right?"

Dammit, I'll go over there if you'll go with me."

"Hell, I can't go. I just signed a three-year contract, and there's no damn way I can get out of it. And they damn sure wouldn't let me go with you over there. You big son of a bitch, you have to take the job. Hell, if you make all that money, and Chicago is one of the best cities in all of baseball. Hell, nobody gets fired over there."

"Okay, if you don't take the damn job, you owe it to your wife and four kids. It ain't for yourself."

Paul Owens worked hard on Dallas to stay. The Phillies needed some continuity now that the Carpenter family had sold the club. He offered Dallas a sizable salary increase, but the Cubs upped the ante to $300,000. Paul and Hughie insisted that Dallas take the job.

Dallas joined the Cubs with a quote, "I'm no Messiah, but I'll guarantee no one will outwork us."

Hopping over to Chicago did not end Dallas's ongoing relationship with his Phillies mates, including trades between the Cubs and Phillies. Hughie, Paul, and Dallas kept the phone lines busy, with rumors spreading about more impending trades. In January 1982 a deal was made. Larry Bowa was traded to the Cubs for shortstop

Ivan DeJesus, and to sweeten the pot, the Phillies threw in a rookie infielder just out of the Oklahoma City farm club, Ryne Sandberg. Dallas got the better part of that deal, a fiery infielder and a future Hall of Famer and ten-time All-Star player.

What comes around turns around. The Phillies got a great deal with Steve Carlton a decade earlier. Now the Cubs got a trump card, a future Hall of Famer virtually free of charge.

24

Looking at Another Scoreboard

During the off-season of 1982, the Owens-Alexander combo got the remaining core of the Big Red Machine of the earlier decade—Pete Rose, Joe Morgan, and Tony Perez. (Rose signed on in 1979.) Perez signed as a free agent and Morgan was traded by the Giants with Al Holland. The Phillies shipped a Minor Leaguer and pitchers Mark Davis and Mike Krukow. The three former Reds had one more hurrah, as it was the last year for the three of them together.

The Phillies had an aging team, but they had a hot September and went on to defeat the Dodgers for the pennant. Owens replaced Pat Corrales as manager and continued trading for immediate help in the outfield and on the mound to be winners in the World Series. Then they stared at the Orioles with pitching standouts Jim Palmer, Scott McGregor, and Tippy Martinez. The Orioles bested the Phillies, four games to one.

For the Phillies the 1983 World Series was a swan song, as they slowly mired themselves in the second division for the remainder of the decade, except for the 1986 season, when they finished in second place but still twenty-one and a half games behind the Mets.

With the Cubs, Dallas Green took on another challenge by rebuilding a club that languished in second division and had last appeared in the World Series in 1938. With only one winning season in ten years, Dallas began rebuilding its farm system and making some trades, getting Larry Bowa and Ryne Sandberg from the Phillies. In early 1984 he got Gary Mathews and Bob Dernier from the Phillies, two trades among many with the Phillies. The club turned around rather quickly, for in 1984 the Cubs won the NL East title, then lost to the Padres in the playoffs. The pennant, ever elusive, seemed to be stamped, "Wait 'til next year."

Dallas and Hughie remained in close contact with one another, discussing trades and talking about the chance to work together again. Wearing different uniforms does not create any barriers in baseball. You have to keep your contacts updated on a monthly basis, if not more often. Approaching trade deadlines and amateur draft picks and bonding with one another are the recipes for success in baseball's front offices.

Finally, in 1987, Hughie joined Dallas in Chicago. Within days of his arrival they sat down, pouring over a list of players to trade to continue the rebuilding effort. To both men it appeared to be a perfectly ordinary thing to do, although some in the front office thought Hughie impulsive in acting so swiftly.

Seeking new talent and finding a marquee player became paramount. The Cubs needed their own twelve-step program, resulting in a tough makeover. Hope and then despair seemed to follow the Cubs for another year and the next ones also offered no hope, as heads rolled and injuries mounted.

Like other scouts, Hughie went through his own learning phases as baseball changed. "Ka-chung" sounded the cash register of baseball economics with the implementation of the draft system, the end of the unconditional reserve clause, and more college graduates entering the game.

The Cubs had developed other ways to evaluate a player's potential, including psychological testing. The front office now required their scouts to look at categories of importance for the fielding positions. A catcher was to be evaluated on his fielding as the number-one priority, followed by arm, hitting power, and running. For a shortstop it was fielding, arm, speed, hitting, and power. In the outfield, the emphasis for the left and right fielders focused on power, hitting, speed, fielding, and arm, in that order, with the center fielder having fielding, speed, hitting, power, and arm.

What did not change? Everybody looked for another left-handed pitcher.

Just after Hughie arrived in early '87, Dallas pulled off one of his top signings. He got a hot player at a bargain-basement price by signing Andre Dawson, who became a free agent after playing with Montreal for eleven years. Dawson's agent, Dick Moss, approached Hughie during spring training in Arizona and asked if he could get an appointment with Dallas. "Yeah, if you're gonna talk about Dawson, then we'll talk."

Dawson was a helluva ballplayer, and it looked like Montreal didn't have enough money to sign him. Dallas called Montreal's general manager and asked him what his top offer was going to be. The Cubs didn't want to get into a bidding war, which they could have easily won. Dallas didn't want to do that. After more talks, Moss pulled out a contract from his pocket and opened it. The spaces for salary and bonuses were blank.

"Dallas, you guys, I'm gonna walk outside, and you guys put a figure down. If you want Dawson, put a figure in that contract, and we'll accept whatever figure you put in there," Moss remarked. Dallas put in $500,000 (actually $500,000 with $200,000 of incentives). Hughie thought for sure they would back off, but Dawson accepted the contract. That was the strangest negotiation Hughie ever witnessed in his career.

Within weeks of arriving in Chicago as a Major League scout and player consultant, Hughie got the job to trade big, left-hander pitcher Steve "Rainbow" Trout to the Yankees. His daddy was Dizzy Trout, who teamed up with Hal Newhouser of the Tigers during the forties and was known for some weird habits on and off the field.

Like father, like son. Steve was goofy, absolutely goofy. That's no exaggerating. He'd do the damndest things; he hit a ball one time and ran to third base, instead of first. He just didn't have any sense.

Early in the '87 season he pitched two consecutive shutouts. Eighteen scoreless innings that goofy SOB pitched. Well, George Steinbrenner got a hold of Hughie after hearing about Trout.

"What would you take for Trout? We need him," Steinbrenner offered.

Hughie knew that Trout couldn't pitch very well, and he knew damn well he couldn't pitch in New York City. In New York the nightclubs stayed open too late. He knew that Trout couldn't pitch there. Both Dallas and Hughie agreed to get rid of Trout while they could. But he had $4 million coming to him.

"Well, if you'd turn me loose on Steinbrenner, I'll get us out of the $4 million," Hughie quickly responded.

"You couldn't do that," Dallas snapped.

"By God, you just watch me. If you'll give me permission . . ." Hughie smelled a deal.

He got the Yankees general manager on the phone to find out if they were still interested in Trout. They were, so the Cubs got three players, including Bob Tewksbury. Steinbrenner picked up the $4 million tab. (Trout bombed in New York City and finally was sent packing to Seattle. Tewksbury never won a game with the Cubs.)

At the end of the 1987 season Dallas resigned, accepting the Yankees managerial job, after the Cubs finished in third place, some twenty-three games behind the division-winning Mets. He had built a fine farm club system that would finally pay dividends in 1989, the year that everybody expected the Mets and everybody else to beat up on the Cubs. The Cubs won the NL Eastern Division title with a 93-69 record but lost to the Giants four games to one in the playoffs. (Dallas's tenure as Yankees manager lasted but one year under "Boss" Steinbrenner.)

Within days of Green's leaving the Cubs, Jim Frey got a phone call from Chicago. Frey, in his first managerial position, took the Royals to the World Series in 1980. A year later he was fired, then joined the

Cubs in 1984 as manager, where he was fired again in mid-1986. Now, with Green's departure, the Cubs wanted Frey to be their new GM.

Hughie and Jim had known one another for a number of years, so there was no need to get used to one another. For Frey the new job was a change of pace. He had spent his entire career wearing a uniform and admitted not knowing a lot about running a front office. All the more reason for depending on a trusted friend like Hughie.

"I was around a lot of Major League scouts, but I trusted Hughie as much or more than any other scout. He had the unique ability, that is, experience and enthusiasm, for the job, and he was already in his seventies. He talked to everybody, he knew everybody, and he had a great desire to make changes," observed Frey. "Most importantly, I trusted him completely. I trusted his judgment. If I didn't know a lot about a player, I trusted Hughie's judgment. Hughie never wrote reports for me. He told me what he thought about a player—fair, good, excellent. I believed him."

The plan to rebuild the Cubs was to get rid of the older, high-priced players and go after younger players with more speed, more defense. Hughie and Jim looked for some talent in their Minor League clubs. They decided to get rid of four or five guys who were making some pretty big money to get control of the payroll as quickly as possible.

The first trade took place in early December when the Cubs traded Lee Smith for short relievers Calvin Schiraldi and Al Nipper. The bullpen needed shoring up.

For the '88 season they brought up rookie infielder Mark Grace and catcher Damon Berryhill, who quickly took away roster slots from veterans Leon "Bull" Durham and Jody Davis. Sophomore hurler Greg Maddux won eighteen games. It looked as if it would be a great season, but after the All-Star break the team floundered, finishing eight games under the .500 mark.

The year 1989—it was Hughie's golden anniversary as a scout. No one else held that record nor signed as many players who played Major League baseball or served under every baseball commissioner.

To commemorate his achievement, Charlie Joseph, the mayor of Seminole, Oklahoma, met with other city officials and community leaders to announce Hugh Alexander Week. Invitations went out to all of Hughie's baseball friends.

It was a cold, icy February night on the Seminole Junior College campus as baseball dignitaries, friends, and relatives gathered to celebrate his fifty years of scouting. Baseball—there's something for everybody! Hughie's blue eyes danced excitedly seeing the outpouring of town folks. The Dallas Greens, the Jack McKeons, and the Jim Freys of baseball arrived in town. The Cubs sent a contingent and commissioned a fifty-year ring in Hughie's honor. The Cubs asked Ed McGregor, a Chicago reporter, to write a tribute titled "Boy, What a Scout." McGregor highlighted Hughie's career, a mother lode of baseball adventures.

High school buddies, boys of all ages who followed him at the high school, the mayor, and city council members packed into the hall. They wanted to hear Hughie's stories, however exaggerated, about growing up in the oil fields, living in the fire hall, galloping around a ball field, and sneaking a few drinks. The old movie theater where Hughie made a few extra bucks a week and the fire hall still stood in silent testimony.

Earlier in the day a few of his high school buddies marched onto the high school football field to re-create his kicking a 60-yard field goal. Did it really happen? It happened, because they thought it did. No one would ever contest the veracity of their stories, not even old salty baseball veterans.

Hughie worked the banquet hall that evening like a politician. His beguiling smile attracted everyone, whatever one's walk of life. Even a cub reporter felt like a Grantland Rice or a Roger Angell after asking Hughie a couple of questions. He let everyone know just how important he was or would be. The word *stranger* held no meaning in his vocabulary.

Sitting back in their chairs, the old-timers listened and remembered the tough days of the Great Depression as they ate dinner.

Ruddy complexions chiseled from years of outdoor work on the windy Oklahoma prairie made for a Norman Rockwell gallery.

Hughie's craggy face and thinning reddish hair marked the only identification of his age. Quite evident were his enduring qualities: inventiveness and persistence. When he spoke in a quiet yet upbeat tone, friends and admirers stopped to listen. Whatever story he remembered, each one embraced his love of baseball. In their presence was a real-life Horatio Alger of baseball. How could anyone not love Hughie, even if he was trying to get the best ballplayer at the lowest price?

After dinner Dallas Green, the master of ceremonies, lumbered up to the microphone. Now the New York Yankees manager, he and Hughie had known one another for over twenty years. When they were with the Phillies they gripped and argued with one another about trading up-and-coming stars. But they knew how to build winners, and just as important, they knew how to be winners.

Dallas began his remarks with a story about inviting Hughie to dinner to his home outside Philadelphia. Days before his arrival, Dallas warned his children not to stare at Hughie's left arm. "He has no hand, but I don't want you kids staring at his stump all evening. Just be polite and pretend nothing is unusual. Mr. Alexander does not think he has any handicap and he doesn't want anybody paying attention to his missing hand. If he wants to tell you kids how it happened, he will."

On cue, the Green children faithfully obeyed their father's orders. After some conversation, they all came to the dining room. Then Mrs. Green entered and with immense culinary pride placed a large platter of steaks on the table. An audible gasp arose, as the children just stared at Hughie. How could a one-handed man cut a T-bone steak? Hughie did it, albeit with some awkwardness. Hughie was up to the task, as he learned years ago that the word *handicapped* appeared only on the golf course and at the race track. Nowhere else.

Upon finishing the story, Dallas remarked, "I'm glad we didn't serve steak tonight."

Jim Frey, manager of the Cubs, talked about rebuilding the team, as it had been eighty years since a World Series victory flag flew over Wrigley Field. He depended on Hughie for advice about every possible trade and about the talent in their Minor League clubs. Yes, when Hughie spoke, the Cubs' front office listened.

Now it was Hughie's turn. The truth about his career would come out, although every story he told began with "it may not exactly happen this way, but that's the way I remember it." So what if some of his stories flirted with the truth. That's baseball! That's the thrill of the moment. Let the audience fill in the details.

Charley Joseph, the mayor of Seminole, called out for the story about a kid from Commerce, Oklahoma, about 125 miles from Seminole. Without hesitation, Hughie leaped into the story.

"In the late spring about 1948, one of the Yankees scouts called me. Would I do him a favor and scout a player playing American Legion ball in Neosho, Missouri? He was busy and couldn't get there. I told him I would do it as a favor, so I hopped on a train to Neosho the next day. I watched the kid for three days, and after the last game I went up to him and introduced myself to him. His name was Mickey Mantle. I wanted to talk with him about professional baseball, but Mickey said his father did the talking for him. I would have to talk with his dad back home.

"I made a note and hopped a train back to Seminole. Awaiting me was a pile of messages from the Yankees scout. 'Why haven't you called me? What did the kid do? Call me.'

"That night I called the scout. 'Well, what did he do, Hughie?'

"Well, I told him that the boy struck out nine times in three games. (I didn't tell him until days later that he also hit nine home runs.) Them Yankees had a lock on him anyway."

John Dawson, a Seminole city councilman, asked Hughie if he remembered his mother and her three sisters. Hughie's eyes glistened, a wide grin grew across his face, and the days of being a ladies' man reappeared. The girls enjoyed dating him but didn't consider him marriage material. Maybe he was simply too handsome and knew how to talk to pretty girls. But he had a quiet side. He never told the sisters that he was dating them all at the same time.

What was evident was that everybody knew Hughie, even if only for a moment. He approached each person as if he were the owner of a ball club. One always felt important around him. And they sought his attention, whether at the ballpark, in a hotel lobby, or in a restaurant.

He did not seek fame. Rather, it simply came to him. Whenever he stopped at a good "watering hole" like Mike Ditka's restaurant in Chicago just to kibitz, football players, movie stars, and politicians moved quickly to his table. Fame came to him casually, and in the same manner, he passed it around to others, whatever their station in life.

It was an evening of laughter, a few tears, and a showering of immense pride on a hometown boy who had made good.

25

History Repeats Itself

History repeated itself. High hopes, great beginning, and then a malaise struck the club. The Cubbies finished in fourth place in the NL East in 1988 with a 77-85 record, twenty-four games behind the Mets. The only truly history-making event for the season—Wrigley Field turned on the lights for night baseball for the first time on August 8, 1988. They beat the Mets.

To build a more competitive team, the Cubs had to make some off-season trades at the end of the season. Hughie had a long and astute working relationship with the Texas Rangers; he knew the front office people and the players. He and Jim Frey made a controversial trade with the Rangers, making tongues wag that the Cubs got duped. Frey was roundly criticized for giving away too much talent for too many unknown players, but Hughie knew that in getting Mitch Williams, he had a fine "short man."

Still, swapping Rafael Palmeiro and pitchers Jamie Moyer and Drew Hall to Texas for pitchers Mitch Williams, Paul Kilgus, and Steve Wilson, infielders Curt Wilkerson and Luis Benetiz, and outfielder Pablo Delgado just didn't make sense to Cubs fans and sportswriters. Palmeiro, who had batted .307, and Moyer, a promising pitcher, were simply too much to give up. Frey took a public beating for giving up veterans for unknown players. No wonder the Cubs held great expectations early in the season, then collapsed.

A predicted fifth-place finish in '89 was all the experts gave the Cubs. But Mitch Williams pulled off one miracle after another, ending with thirty-six saves. Mike Bielecki had eighteen victories when he had won only twelve games in his entire career. Jerome Walton, rookie of the year, batted safely in thirty consecutive games. Maddux finished with a 19-12 season; Sutcliffe won sixteen.

Shawon Dunston, Mark Grace, and Ryne Sandberg carried the offense with Luis Salazar as bench strength. The Cubs clinched the 1989 NL East crown to celebrate Wrigley Field's seventy-fifth anniversary season. But the miracle season ended with the Giants beating them in five games for the NL pennant.

Within a couple of months after the 1989 season began, Hughie heard a rumor in the Houston press box that it was a damn shame that Russ Nixon, manager of the Braves, didn't like Paul Assenmacher. He wanted to give him away. Smelling a trade to beef up the pitching corps, Hughie hustled back to the airport to get a flight to Atlanta. The next morning he rushed to the ballpark to talk with Bobby Cox, then the Braves general manager.

"Is Assenmacher available?" Hughie asked.

"You damn right he is. Why don't you and I go up to my office?"

As the game got underway, they started talking, a lot of talking. Cox wanted three players for Assenmacher. After more talking, the Cubs finally agreed to give him Rick Luecken and Pat Gomez. Close to midnight, they still were at the ballpark negotiating. Bobby wanted a Minor Leaguer named Garcia.

At 2:00 a.m. Hughie got on the phone with Frey. Frey gave him the go sign. "I got the okay to make the trade, Bobby. Have Assenmacher ready in the morning."

Hughie unequivocally believed he was the best scout in baseball and deserved a bonus. Even Frey couldn't figure out how Hughie had pulled off the deal.

"Assenmacher will be here at 11:00 a.m. Pick him up at the airport and pitch him today if you have to," boasted Hughie.

Within twenty-four hours of Hughie's arrival in Chicago, Frey took him aside. "That was a helluva job."

You know what Assenmacher did with the Cubs in '89. He posted a 1.46 ERA. Every time afterward when he saw Hughie, he came up to shake hands. "Hey, Hughie, thanks for making me a millionaire."

"Where are you going now?" Frey asked Hughie.

"I'm going to San Diego this afternoon to see my good friend Jack McKeon, the manager of the Padres. I'm gonna get Luis Salazar and Marvell Wynne."

"Well, you might get Wynne, because he's an extra outfielder."

"The reason I want him is in case something happens to our center fielder," replied Hughie, knowing that the trading deadline was nearing.

Frey remarked, "You can't get Salazar 'cause he's the big favorite out there."

"I don't give a damn how big a favorite he is. He's thirty-five years old and I'll get him, even if I have to get him on loan. I'll get him."

The next morning Hughie called Jack McKeon at his home. "Jack, this is Hughie, I want to sit down and visit with you."

Hughie and Jack had known one another since Jack's days as manager of the Kansas City Royals in the early seventies. Of course, everybody in baseball knew Uncle Hughie. Hughie was with the Phillies at that time, and when they got together, making a trade was the first thing on their agenda. They became good friends during the next fifteen years, passing on information about players.

By 2:00 p.m. Hughie was in Jack's office in San Diego. He had to talk fast, because at 4:30 the Padres took batting practice. (A year earlier, in 1988, the Padres fired Larry Bowa and Jack became both general manager and manager.)

"Dammit, Hughie, I'll give you Wynne, but Salazar is a big favorite out here because he's from Mexico, right across the border."

"I don't give a damn how popular he is. I need him in the worst way. I can win the pennant if I can get him."

Finally Jack relented. "Okay, you're a friend of mine, and we can help your club, if you need a third baseman real bad. But I gotta have three players."

Jack picked up the phone to talk with Frey. "I don't know if I should do this, but I'll go ahead and sign the deal. But you gotta promise if you get in the pennant race, you gotta help me."

"Okay, we'll trade you Calvin Schiraldi [pitcher], outfielder Darrin Jackson, and a kid playing over in Japan, Phil Stephenson."

The next day Salazar reported to the Cubs, and they won the game in the bottom half of the tenth inning with a triple. (In the game on the preceding day, Assenmacher saved it in relief.)

Salazar and Wynne had great September numbers. It was a helluva trade, and Salazar stayed for four more years.

That was Hughie's recipe for success. If not a general manager in name, he knew what clubs wanted to trade which players. Jack McKeon became part of the pipeline. They talked to one another once or twice a week, never afraid to tell one another what each needed for his club.

Trust—that is what they had. Jack knew that whatever he talked about, Hughie would never use it against him. Whatever was said, it wouldn't go any further. Each wanted the other to be a winner in any trades, unlike some of their contemporaries who wanted a Mercedes while giving up a Ford Pinto. It was because of that mutual trust that in 1983, with Jack as general manager of the Padres, Hughie called him from Philadelphia. The Phillies were in the pennant race and needed a fleet-footed outfielder, namely Sixto Lezcano of the Padres.

The trading deadline arrived with the Padres playing the Phillies in a night game. (In those days a club had to "deliver" a traded ballplayer physically to the other club. Just announcing a trade did not culminate the agreement.) As the game was played, Jack and his staff huddled with Bill Giles, Hughie, and a couple of others to work a trade.

The clock hit 9:00 p.m. with no deal settled.

"I want this guy and that other guy!" Jack demanded.

"Nope, you can't have them," Giles replied.

The negotiations continued for a couple more hours. Finally, Jack told his people, "Let's get out of here. We can't negotiate with these guys."

Up popped Hughie. "Wait a minute! Wait a minute! Bill, let's go into another office and talk about this."

Off they went. Hughie told Giles, "Jack needs some sweetener, or he'll walk out of here."

Returning about 11:15 p.m., Giles offered a Double-A Minor Leaguer to make the trade. "This kid will be a six-year free agent at the end of the year," Jack retorted.

"No, he's not," shouted one of the Phillies staff.

"Like hell he isn't, go check your records," Jack hollered.

Hurriedly, they poured through the personnel file. Yes, he was a six-year free agent.

Finally, after another meeting, the Phillies agreed on another Minor Leaguer. At 11:50 p.m. the Padres walked Lezcano over to the Phillies' dugout. They delivered the man ten minutes before the deadline.

A few days later Hughie and Jack met in a hotel lobby. "You know, Jack, Bill Giles said that you knew our players better than we did." (The Padres got five players; the Phillies got Steve Fireovid.)

Sometimes to get a player you have to overpay the other club, especially when you're in a pennant stretch. It's the perennial tug-of-war between player development and trading for a veteran who will make a difference. You have to trade youngsters for a veteran who can help the club immediately. And it helps if a club has a lot of good Minor League players. You can trade some of them because you always have just a few roster slots open each year.

Jack always credited Hughie as the one who was instrumental in getting the deal. Without him, it would not have been made.

The Phillies made it to the World Series in 1983, the second time in four years.

During their tenure together with the Cubs, Uncle Hughie and Jim Frey had a rapport probably unlike any other scout and general manager. Frey talked with Hughie almost daily. When Hughie talked, Frey took notes. When they went out to the ballpark together, they didn't take stopwatches or radar guns or a computer like the young guys. All those gadgets looked like a charade when judging talent.

The young, inexperienced scouts have grown up with high-tech gadgets. They have used reams of paper tallying numbers and percentages, but many of them don't know what kind of ballplayer they are looking at. Of course, the fans love the stats, as do the sportswriters. That's what sells newspapers and fantasy baseball.

So what if a guy can throw a ball at 95 mph. If he doesn't know the game, he'll sit on the bench. He has to know the game instinctively. He has to have baseball intelligence. A good scout knows how to put the tools of the trade together with a kid's courage and toughness. You don't find those things with a stopwatch and radar gun.

Jim remarked, "I just didn't know if I trust somebody who gives me a book full of stats—stacks of paper. What am I to do with all that shit? Stats are good at the end of the year for fans and sportswriters looking at what a player has accomplished. But unless you know a guy's heart and his makeup, his courage, they aren't worth shit. What can't be put into stats is a player's intelligence for baseball—intelligence for playing in the Major Leagues."

Years later, Frey reminisced about working with Hughie.

"I used to go to the ballpark with just a matchbox and a pencil in my pocket, just like Hughie. I listed a few players. If I didn't like a player, I put an *X* beside his name. The ones I like got a check mark. That ones I really liked got an asterisk after watching them five, six, seven times. I had a good idea who could be a decent player, a pretty good player, and a star."

During his years with the Cubs Hughie spent his time thinking about another trade to build the team. What was happening in any given ball game was no longer the top priority. He would watch a game, but his mind was about making a trade tomorrow. If he got turned down on one trade, he kept trying to figure out what he had to come back with, hopefully to get a better player.

Baseball is like a giant recycling bin, making the old new with the scent of freshness. An addition to the roster generates a hope for greater certainty. Certainty in any business is an illusion, but it is still a thrill to pursue it.

By the early nineties much of Hughie's time was spent advising Larry Hines, now the Cubs' general manager, about ballplayers with other clubs who might help the Cubs. (Larry had previously been the general manager of the White Sox.) Just before the '92 season began, the White Sox thought they could win the pennant with another power hitter. They looked uptown at George Bell.

Bell could really hit, but he couldn't do anything else. Maybe a trade was in the offering. Hines had gotten Sammy Sosa from the Rangers in '89, and he saw Sosa to be a good, young player. He had a good arm, could run, and could hit the ball five hundred feet. Both Larry and Hughie knew that he was really a strikeout hitter. You talk about strikeouts; he just didn't have any patience up at the plate.

Hughie recommended that Larry make the trade now. "Bell is about finished," he said. The trade was made that quickly and simply.

When Sammy Sosa arrived in the Cubs camp in 1992, he had matured. Hughie remembered a game Sosa played during a short stint in the Minors with Des Moines. He struck out four times and missed the balls by a foot. Hughie took him aside and talked about having more patience at the plate.

"Right now the pitchers are laughing at you. They know how to strike you out. They're going to throw you two bad fastballs clear out of the strike zone, and then they're going to throw you a breaking ball that's going to miss the plate about a foot or so and you're going to swing. Another strikeout," Hughie put it bluntly, yet caringly.

Sosa got better because he was dedicated, but Hughie had no idea he was going to hit that well. By '96 and '97 he came into his own. He was one of the best kids Hughie had been around. He just worked hard. Damn, he'd come out at three in the afternoon and have the players and coaches look at him and see what he was doing right or wrong.

There was one month with the Cubs when he fell into a deep slump. He couldn't hit anything. In one game he hit a couple of ground balls and pop-ups, and he didn't run to first base. He just sort of trotted.

The next day Hughie asked the manager if he could come out early the next day and talk with Sammy in the dugout, not out on the field. "Sammy, you're my boy! You know when you hit those ground balls last night and that pop fly that you didn't run to first base? Do you remember that?"

"Yep," he replied. "I was just mad at myself."

"Well, do you know how many scouts were sitting up behind home plate? And they all had a watch on you. You really looked like horse shit running down to first base. Every one of those scouts made a little note in their book what you looked like. It'll go down for the rest of your life; it will be in somebody's book that you don't . . . that you loaf. It doesn't make any difference where you hit the damn ball now, you just run as fast as you can. You love the game. You got a good arm."

During his last year with the Cubs, Hughie found himself remembering what Slapnicka and Rickey taught him after signing a player. You got to stick with him, to encourage him when he gets down on himself. That is what is to be expected.

Up in the grandstand the fan wants to see the unexpected, a remarkable time at bat, another thrill of a double play. Never does he see the invisible corps of scouts who brought the players from the sandlots to the Big Show. That's the way it is and will always be.

26

Overcoming Pitfalls in
Seeking Certainty

After sixty years of scouting, Hughie hung up his car keys, his scouting reports, and his droopy, weather-beaten hat in 1998. His health was failing. The hacking cough betrayed the cancer eating away at his lungs, but giving up cigarettes at this stage of his life was out of the question. He spent much of his time tendering his ranch north of Brooksville, Florida. The gentle, rolling, green pasture slowly undulated in the late October sun. At the far southern reaches of the ranch, horses leisurely trotted while a newborn foal gamely caught up with its mother. Nearby, a few head of Holsteins lay on the ground gathering up the warmth of the sun. Only the sound of a screeching hawk interrupted the quietness.

A mellowness covered the deeply furrowed wrinkles in Hughie's sun-parched face. His reddish hair, thinned by age, sprayed in several directions. Someone once remarked that his face looked like a sun-bleached urchin. Hard-nosed but with a disarming smile, he greeted any competitor or friend with a warm hello. Within a few moments the person felt as if he had just sat down to renew an acquaintance interrupted by several years. Plainspoken and absorbing, Hughie reduced life's experiences from the complicated to the elementary in the same manner as he described baseball.

Uncle Hughie loved to visit with anyone, be he a batboy, owner, coach, player, or manager, telling stories about the players he signed and the ones that got away. He began talking about the yesteryears, recalling the road maps leading to ballparks, with stops along the way at beer joints, pool halls, and countless homes. Dirt roads and two-lane asphalt highways led to another game on another day.

In 1998 Hughie was battling cancer, but he never mentioned the big "C." His handshake remained firm, his smile and dancing blue eyes were unaffected by disease. He picked up another cigarette, lit it, paused, and began spinning another story about a journeyman ballplayer and an "up and coming" scout.

Sixty years as a scout. Sixty years hawking his brand of baseball, whether with one hand or two. He overcame any fear early in life. Getting hit by a 90-mph fastball is not comparable to getting into a ring with a 250-pound, half-crazed boxer. To a rookie complaining about cold weather and greasy food, he retorted, "Try driving a car without power steering hundreds of thousands of miles with one arm and a stub."

He speculated about baseball with the coming of the new millennium and wondered if pitchers would return to dominance in the game after a decade of home run hitting spiked with steroids and other drugs. Reflected in his tone and words but difficult to capture was his caring about people who loved baseball. He cared about the men, however painful their punctured dreams, not to be fulfilled.

Whenever the topic of baseball statistics arose, his brow furrowed and a few expletives popped out of his mouth. "What do statistics tell you?" he asked rhetorically. "Just a bunch of guys sitting around and gossiping about RBIs, HRs, SBs, and OBPs. But that tells only part of the baseball story. Those guys count *what* happened, not *why* or *when* it happened. I didn't believe in all these numbers. I didn't use a radar gun or calculators. Who knows even if the guns are accurate anyway?"

Hughie remained skeptical about statistics, especially when people started using them to predict the outcome of a ball game. Besides, numbers bounce around from one week to another. A statistician might say that statistics do not reveal causation, only correlation.

Stats do not even try to measure the impact of a player in the dugout, yet in the nineties statistics were put into a lot of contracts. For Hughie, when he started professional baseball in the midthirties, there was only one statistic in a contract—the salary.

Hughie used his judgment with a measure of luck to predict how a player would perform three years hence. It was his practical expertise.

At least they got to play the game. He felt deeply about the way a player hustled down the line and how a player respected the field when he stepped onto the infield for the first time. What he wanted to see in a hustling player, he demanded from himself—playing the game as if his life depended on it, caressing the game yet punching at it, loving its traditions yet bridling at its barriers.

Print does not do justice to the experience of having the opportunity to sit and listen to Hughie's tales about the men of baseball. He loved baseball because the game has high expectations. The bar's high—that's the way it should be. What would you rather have—a place where nobody cares?

Did his passion for the game begin with the loss of his left hand? Before the accident, he knew he was damn good. God gave him the talent to do anything on the field. He played like the one in charge of every game's outcome. Slaps on the back, accolades, and newspaper headlines confirmed his beliefs.

"Danny, those kids have to have a burning gut feeling to be ballplayers. I don't care how much talent they have. To get to the Big Show, they had to prove themselves. I always asked a kid, 'So you want to be a ballplayer. You got ten thousand hours to do it, to make a play or a hit look so simple that anyone in the stands thinks he can do it?'"

Uncle Hughie, by his own account, signed sixty-three players who made it to the Big Show, beginning with Allie Reynolds and Dale Mitchell. Others on his list to sign got away, much to his chagrin. Sixty years later, in 1998, he proudly said, "Well, I've hit the circuit. I've been lucky. I've been a groomsman for over sixty years, leading guys down the aisle to the big leagues. I've served under every baseball commissioner from Judge Landis to Bud Selig. Every one of the five clubs I worked for was a winner, whether rebuilding itself or fighting for a World Series ring." (Three of his teams played in the World Series: the Indians [1948], the Dodgers [1956, 1959, 1963, 1964, 1966], and the Phillies [1980, 1983].)

Some folks are smart enough to enjoy a delightful and challenging moment in their lives. They recall, "It happens only *once*." Hughie had lots of "onces" in his life. Once he was a promising ballplayer; then he became baseball's first super scout. Once he wondered if he would simply be a spectator, watching other people make things happen; then he decided to make things happen.

Scouting is not rocket science; neither is playing baseball. Charlie Fox, a scout for over forty-five years, once observed in the *Sporting News*, "For the batter, it's still 'See the ball, hit the ball.' For the fielder, it's still 'Catch the ball, throw the ball.' For the pitcher, it's still 'Throw strikes, but don't give him anything good to hit.'"

The fundamental work of scouts is "digging out raw talent in the first place," said Leonard Koppett in *The Thinking Man's Guide to Baseball*. A scout has to make a judgment call about a player's abilities in the next five to ten years. Because so much money is involved in bonuses and multiyear contracts, a scout looks for players who have the right mechanics and a well-honed work ethic.

For the scout, it's training the eye to see what others don't see in a ballplayer. He works and works, breaking down the simple acts of swinging a bat or fielding a grounder. There's nothing innate about a scout's abilities. It's practicing the right things for thousands of hours. It's only a game, but it takes a lot of sweat, preparation, and dedication by scouts and ballplayers.

Like other scouts, Hughie sought certainty in an illusionary business. He often remarked that there is a very thin line between success and failure. You can go and look at a high school or college kid who has all the ability in the world, get him in the draft, and when he goes out and plays, he finds twenty-five thousand fans in the grandstand, not one hundred. Then he gets the shakes.

The trump card is figuring out what is going on inside a young man's head. His attitudes, his determination to shrug off any failures and focus on the next ground ball or pitch—that is what counts. Find a RAT to sign. Find a kid who is Reliable, has the right Attitude, and with Talent.

In baseball with all the money on the muscle, everybody wants instant results. That's the name of the game. No longer does a hot prospect spend five years in the Minors. Too much money is at stake. There is constant pressure to bring him up in a hurry. The owner wants a quick return on the bonus. The fans want to see the next Sammy Sosa and Josh Beckett.

But mastery is still ten thousand hours away, even if a kid is a natural athlete. Being Major League talent takes hard, hard work. It's about discipline and perseverance and the desire to be different. The rookie who displays these qualities and does not get injured is the one most likely to succeed.

One of the biggest tests of a young man is when he fails or goes into a slump. Does the strikeout at the last time at bat stick in his head, or did he analyze what pitches were thrown during the last time at bat? Ballplayers need short memories, remembering only the mistake they made in the last inning so that it doesn't happen again.

What a good scout does, especially with marginal players, reflects the belief that perseverance and a strong work ethic trump a missing tool of the trade. He looks at a kid and knows he doesn't have all the ability but says, "Let's give him a chance to play, because he goes out and plays hard. With his winning attitude, he overcomes obstacles and becomes a good big league player."

Hughie detested being invisible or boring. Scouting, in his view, was an extrovert's paradise and an introvert's challenge. He was the extrovert and talked baseball to anyone who loved the game. For those interested in becoming a manager or scout, he made the game real, spending hours reeling off stories laden with advice. Lucky is the person who gets to hear someone share his love and passion about his life's pursuit.

"I roar like a lion, because for too many years scouts have been hidden from view." He loved a deal and expected to be around the table persuading and cajoling with general managers and farm club directors about why or why not a certain player should be signed or traded.

If money, trading, and player development are the lifeblood of baseball, then scouting is its cardiovascular system. An effective scout is looking for the pulse of the next good player, well aware that hundreds of other scouts are doing the same thing.

In the last few years of his life, Hughie's career took a turn down another road. He encouraged young men who love the game to become scouts. Many dropped by his ranch; others called him on the phone, asking his advice about hot prospects and how to deal with pressure from the front office. Gladly and freely, Hughie offered his full attention to them so that another generation could find the talent to fill a club's roster.

He simply loved the game of baseball. He lived a life out loud—exhilarating, driven, and calculating. If lyrics can capture his personality, they are those of Dory Previn from the song "You're Gonna Hear from Me":

Move over, sun, and give me some sky
I got me some wings I'm eager to try
I may be unknown but wait till I've flown
You're gonna hear from me.

Hundreds of baseball people heard from and about Uncle Hughie. A street fighter and a loveable cuss, he wove magical webs around anyone who dared enter his life.

Hughie died on November 25, 2000, after a short illness, in Oklahoma City. He is buried next to his parents and sister in Maple Grove Cemetery in Seminole, Oklahoma.

Uncle Hughie was a horse-trader playing in baseball's future markets while sitting in the grandstand reciting the lore of the game. He carried no radar gun or stopwatch. A pencil and a pad of paper were just fine, and even then he took few notes. "A scout after fifty years of experience should be able to decide whether or not a ballplayer has the talent and attitude to make it."

A year after his death the movie *Summer Catch* was released. It was about a local baseball prospect who gets an opportunity to play in the Cape Cod Baseball League for the Chatham Athletics. John C. McGinley appeared in the role of Hugh Alexander.

During my eight years with Hughie, I reflected on the qualities that made Hughie unique: cunning as a fox, persuasive as a preacher, gripping as a storyteller, joyful simply to be around.